A Time for Weeping
Biblical Wisdom for Those who Suffer.

A Time for Weeping
Biblical Wisdom for Those who Suffer.

Scott Higgins

JUST FAITH

Copyright © 2016 Scott Higgins

Title: A Time for Weeping. Biblical Wisdom for Those Who Suffer

Author: Scott Higgins

ISBN: 9780992425746

ALL RIGHTS RESERVED. This book is copyright. Apart from any fair dealing for the purposes of private study, research, criticism or review, as permitted under the Copyright Act no part of this book may be reproduced or transmitted in any form or by any means, electronic or mechanical, including photocopying, recording, or by any information storage and retrieval system without express written permission from the author/publisher.

Scripture, unless otherwise stated, taken from the New Revised Standard Version Bible: Anglicized Edition, copyright © 1989, 1995 National Council of the Churches of Christ in the United States of America. Used by permission. All rights reserved.

All interior paper stock is acid-free and supplied by a Forest Stewardship Council (FSC) certified provider. We are committed to recycling waste materials resulting from the printing process and only produce units as they are ordered, which reduces excess production

To Sandy,
My beloved partner in life,
Whose generous love, extraordinary patience,
And willingness to walk life's journey with me
never ceases to humble me and fill me with joy.

Contents

Introduction	1
Jesus. The Key to Living with Suffering	4
Hagar. God Sees Me	19
Psalms. Screaming at God	33
Job. The Limits of Wisdom	43
Qoholet. Enjoy the Sunshine While You Can	58
Ruth. The Welcoming Arms of Community	69
Paul. The Fringe Benefits of Suffering	80
John. The Final Healing	91

Introduction

I was eighteen years old when I delivered my first sermon at my home church. I elected to preach on the sovereignty of God and spent weeks researching, reflecting and writing. In the week leading up to the sermon a woman who belonged to our church was brutally murdered. When I stood up to preach I felt sick in the stomach. How could anyone believe what I had to say in light of her death? How could I believe it? What did it mean to say that God was in control when events like this occurred?

Years later I became a pastor and discovered that many people found life difficult. At any given time around 20% to 25% of households in our church were undergoing some kind of crisis. It could be the loss of a job, a sexual assault, a debilitating illness, severe depression, a terminally ill child, or any one of a number of other challenges to well-being. While everybody else seemed to carry on as though all was good with the world, for these households the world had stopped spinning. They knew heartache, anxiety, and uncertainty.

My own experience has been a journey with Parkinson's disease and leukemia. Diagnosed with both diseases in 2011, I grow more disabled by the day. I have discovered that faith is not a ticket to freedom from crises and problems, but that it is a source of wisdom, comfort and hope.

When we, or someone we love, suffers two sets of questions are raised. First are the questions to do with the philosophical problem of suffering. How can suffering exist in a universe with a God who is all-good, all-powerful and all-wise? If God is all-good he would want to eliminate suffering; if God is all-powerful he would have the ability to do so; and if God is all-wise he would know the way to achieve it. With this set of questions we are seeking an intellectually coherent explanation of suffering. Through the centuries theologians and philosophers have provided all kinds of answers to this philosophical conundrum. They employ rigorous logic to help us understand how it is coherent to speak of a loving God in a painful world. Such work is important to show that faith is possible.

And then there is the pastoral problem of suffering. How do we live well in the midst of suffering? What does it mean to trust in God? Where do we find a sense of purpose and meaning? With this set of questions we are seeking ways to live meaningfully and to resolve our conflicted emotions.

It is this second set of questions that is the focus of this short work. My goal is to explore the wisdom of the Scriptures for living well in the midst of suffering. We begin with Jesus, whose life, death and resurrection provides the framework by which Christians understand suffering. From there we move back to the Old Testament, beginning with the story of a runaway servant girl who discovers that God "sees" her in the midst of her pain. From Job we learn to trust God even when we fail to understand why we suffer. Turning to the Psalms we discover that the prayer of those who suffer is often the prayer of protest, bewilderment, and even anger at God. From the Teacher in the book of Ecclesiastes we're encouraged to receive the small joys in life as the gift of God, and in the story of Ruth to embrace the healing arms of a welcoming community. Returning to the New Testament, the apostle Paul helps us see the fringe benefits of suffering, that it can be a vehicle for our growth and an opportunity to experience the power of God. We finish with the glorious vision of John in the book of Revelation, the assurance that suffering will not be the last word in the universe. Rather those of us who suffer live with the hope of a final and ultimate healing.

Chapter One

Jesus. The Key to Living with Suffering

2011 was not the best year I have had. It began with a diagnosis that I have Parkinson's disease and concluded with the news that I also have chronic Leukemia. Parkinson's means my brain isn't absorbing enough dopamine, a chemical that allows muscles to be controlled. I have a tremor and stiffness of muscle that started in my right side, is becoming more pronounced, and has recently spread to the left side of my body. The constant tremoring creates a dull ache in my muscles and joints. Tasks that require fine motor skills, such as doing up the button on my shirt-sleeve, pulling on socks, and turning down my collar are becoming increasingly difficult. If I go to dinner with friends my hands can tremor so badly that the cutlery I hold clinks in rapid staccato against the plate and I need to ask a dinner companion to cut up my food. Late at night after my medications have worn off and when I rise in the morning I have to concentrate with all my might to lift my feet off the ground as I walk. The alternative is to slowly shuffle. Some days the meds wear off more rapidly than others and I find myself out in public unable to walk more than 50 metres. My handwriting has become illegible, not only to others but even to myself. I can only drive short distances (after an hour in the car I tend to nod off) and only when my meds have fully kicked in.

I have spent my life as a public communicator, but this is becoming increasingly problematic. I am unable to walk around a stage gesturing like I once used to and my face is becoming increasingly expressionless. Where I once threw myself into my work I now have to pace my days. The constant tremoring uses up energy, which means I grow weary. Sometimes my legs are so stiff I cannot do much but lie down for most of the day.

There is no known cure for Parkinson's. At present the best medicine can do is alleviate some of the symptoms. As the disease continues its spread in my body the technologies will become increasingly less effective. I will continue to deteriorate until I reach a point where I won't be able to dress myself, toilet myself or feed myself. I will reach a point where I will struggle to swallow food, which will set up the conditions in which I will likely contract a form of pneumonia that will cause my death. It is highly likely I will be relatively young when I die.

Leukemia is a cancer that sees my white blood cells multiplying. In my case the increase is incremental and may not require treatment for many years, but like a time-bomb it is ticking away inside my body. It will be a race with time to see which gets me first, the Parkinson's or the Leukemia.

I am not the only one affected by my diseases. In many ways the world has turned upside down for my wife Sandy. We've massively revised our plans for the future, our financial well-being has been detrimentally impacted, and Sandy not only has the pain of watching somebody she loves deteriorate but faces a future in which she will be a full-time carer for somebody with a severe disability and most likely will be widowed at a relatively young age.

At some stage, most of us feel significant pain. We, or someone we love, will experience a debilitating illness; a period of unemployment; a violent assault; a mental disorder; the breakdown of a relationship; or some other life challenge. This will inevitably turn our world upside down, plunge us into the unwelcome process of grieving and its various stages of denial, anger, sadness, bargaining, and acceptance, and things will never be the same for us again.

Christians are not immune to this. We follow a suffering Saviour who warned that difficulties will come our way. But we do have an incredible resource to help us live well through suffering: our faith and the God we proclaim.

At the centre of Christian faith is Jesus, whose life, death and resurrection form a framework through which we can view life and suffering. In the death of Jesus we learn that suffering is a reality in the broken world in which we live; in the resurrection of Jesus we discover the incredible hope that suffering will not be the final word but that God will recreate our hearts, minds, bodies, communities, and even the creation itself; and in the life of Jesus we see how to live meaningfully even when suffering is part of our experience.

Living with Suffering

Jesus lived an exceptionally good life, overflowing in love for God and people. The Gospels are filled with stories of Jesus's transformational impact on people. A woman caught in adultery is delivered from a cruel death by stoning. A crazed man who spent years chained in a cemetery is released from the demons that drove him insane. A woman whose scandalous reputation saw her vilified, mocked and pushed to the margins, is shown welcome and love. He heals multitudes of their infirmities. The blind see, the lame walk, and lepers are made whole. He brings the promise of God's forgiving embrace to those who thought themselves beyond it. Wherever he went he brought grace, healing and hope. Yet at every point he faced strident criticism and violent opposition.

When Jesus was a child, Herod sought his death, forcing Jesus and his parents to flee to Egypt (Matthew 2). When he began his public ministry some thirty years later he remained the focus of violence. The religious establishment claimed he was possessed by demons and conspired to kill him (Matthew 12:24; Mark 11:18). The people of his hometown of Nazareth grew so furious with Jesus that they "drove him out of the town, and led him to the brow of the hill on which their town was built, so that they might hurl him off the cliff" (Luke 4:29). Herod Antipas, drunk with power and perceiving Jesus as a threat, ordered his assassination (Luke 13:31).

These murderous intentions reached their denouement in Jesus's violent death. Betrayed by one of his friends and abandoned by the others, he was convicted on trumped up charges, whipped, beaten, spat upon, mocked, then subject to the most cruel and humiliating form of execution known to the ancient world.

The emotional enormity of these events weighed heavily upon Jesus. The night of his arrest he prayed alone on the Mount of Olives, so anguished that the Gospel writer says "his sweat was like drops of blood falling to the ground" (Luke 22:43). Later, as he hung upon the cross, he cried the words of all those who feel abandoned by God: "My God, my God, why have you forsaken me?"

If the experience of Jesus teaches us anything it is that we do not live in a Pollyanna universe where good things happen to good people and bad things happen to bad people. Rather we live in a universe where we experience both immeasurable delights and gut-wrenching suffering; where people perform heroic acts of service and commit terrible acts of violence; where we experience the good order God placed in the world and tragic accidents; where nature's beauty fills our senses and natural disasters rob people of their lives, their livelihoods and their homes; where we enjoy the freedom of functioning bodies and the distress of shocking diseases that ravage the bodies and minds of people we love. If the Son of God experienced both the joy and the sorrow of life, his followers can expect it too.

Sometimes the prime cause of our suffering will be the actions of others. The apostle Peter spoke to this in the first letter that bears his name. Many in the early Christian community were slaves. While some had masters who were kind and considerate, others had masters who were brutal. A confronting example is found in Diodorus Sicilus who, in the century before Christ, described the lot of slaves in the mining industry:

> *The men engaged in these mining operations produce unbelievably large revenues for their masters... But because of their extremely bad conditions, the mortality rate is high; they are not allowed to give up working or have a rest, but are forced by the beatings of their supervisors to stay at their places and throw away their wretched lives as a result of these horrible hardships. Some of them survive to endure their misery for a long time because of their physical stamina or she will power; but because of the extent of their suffering, they prefer dying to surviving.*
> *Diodorus* 38.1

Peter urges slaves with harsh masters to respond with patient submission, remembering that Christ suffered in a similar manner before them.

> *... if you endure when you do right and suffer for it, you have God's approval. For to this you have been called, because Christ also suffered for you, leaving you an example, so that you should follow in his steps.*
> 1 Peter 2:20 NRSV

The early Christian community found itself experiencing periods of persecution, sometimes at the hands of the State and at other times in a less formal form from their neighbours. The most extreme example comes in the Book of Revelation where the State is depicted as a monstrous, demonic beast intent on waging war on the people of God.

Persecution like this arose because the first century Greco-Roman world was one where people took seriously the idea that the favour of the gods was necessary to keep their cities safe from invading armies and to grant prosperity. When Christians refused to worship the gods they were regarded as a threat to the wellbeing of the city. Moreover, when the Roman Emperor was presented as a god, refusal to worship him was an act of rebellion that demanded swift retribution.

On other occasions we suffer due to the malfunctioning of our bodies and our environment: genes trigger debilitating disease; cancerous cells rapidly multiply; tsunamis, earthquakes, and floods wreak havoc. The apostle Paul speaks to this in Romans chapter 8, where he described the creation as subject to bondage to decay, longing for the day when it will be set free.

> *I consider that the sufferings of this present time are not worth comparing with the glory about to be revealed to us. For the creation waits with eager longing for the revealing of the children of God; for the creation was subjected to futility, not of its own*

> *will but by the will of the one who subjected it, in hope that the creation itself will be set free from its bondage to decay and will obtain the freedom of the glory of the children of God. We know that the whole creation has been groaning in labour pains until now; and not only the creation, but we ourselves, who have the first fruits of the Spirit, groan inwardly while we wait for adoption, the redemption of our bodies. For in hope we were saved. Now hope that is seen is not hope. For who hopes for what is seen? But if we hope for what we do not see, we wait for it with patience.*
> Romans 8:18-25 NRSV

We can also suffer as a result of our own foolishness and sin. Judas was filled with such grief and anguish at his betrayal of Jesus that he committed suicide. The apostle Peter broke down after his repeated denials that he knew Jesus. In Romans 1:18-32 the apostle Paul described the unfolding of God's wrath in terms of people experiencing the depraved depths and consequences of their own evil.

Whether it be self-inflicted, nature-inflicted, or other-inflicted, for Jesus and those of his era suffering was a reality of life. Life was difficult and the notion that Christians would not share in this is foreign to the teaching of Jesus and the New Testament.

Living Faithfully Through Suffering

Left to nothing but the experiences of life and the dictates of logic people reach different conclusions about the shape of reality. Some of us look at the complexity of forces that enable the universe and life to exist, at the beauty of the world, at the longing in our hearts for transcendence and conclude that life is the gift of a wise and powerful God. Others observe the imperfections in nature, the pain in the natural world, and the capacity of human beings for savagery and decide there can be no God, not one of love and wisdom anyway. Yet others sit on the fence, uncommitted either way.

This ambiguity is overcome by revelation. For Christians the pinnacle of revelation is the person of Jesus, in whom God was fully present. In Jesus we discover that God is neither absent nor indifferent. Rather, God is right here with us in the midst of the glory and the messiness of life. God weeps for us, just as Jesus wept for his friend Lazarus and for the beloved city of Jerusalem; God is angered by the callous disregard we can have for each other, just as Jesus was angered at those who opposed his doing good on the Sabbath; God is filled with a love that longs deeply for us, just as Jesus longed for the well-being of his community. God, taught Jesus, is like a father welcoming home a long lost son; like a shepherd searching for every lost sheep; like a woman scouring every corner of her home for a lost coin, and refusing to give up until the coin is found.

If the story of Jesus teaches me that suffering is part of the reality of life, it also teaches me that a God of love is the defining centre of reality, and that in ways I may find difficult to comprehend I am treasured by God.

Living Meaningfully Through Suffering

In this age of consumerism, we tend to define the good life in terms of the ability to enjoy an ever expanding range of goods, services and experiences and to do this in the company of people we love and who love us. Suffering represents the antithesis of this. It is the great enemy of the consumerist vision of the good life.

By this measure Jesus did not enjoy a good life. The three years of his life to which we have access were marked by homelessness, conflict, and a violent end. Yet Christian conviction is that Jesus not only lived a good life, he lived the most purposeful life of any human being in history.

Jesus defined the good life in terms of love for God and love for others. To know oneself to be loved by God, to reciprocate that love and extend it to others was the essence of what it meant to be human. From Jesus we learn that while suffering may be unwelcome and painful, it does not prevent us from living a fully human and fully meaningful life. For as long as we have the capacity to encounter God's love and return it, or to encounter the love of others and return it, we're living into and out of our humanity.

Suffering of course introduces ambiguity into life. Atheist scientist Richard Dawkins captured it this way

> *The total amount of suffering per year in the natural world is beyond all decent contemplation. During the minute that it takes me to compose this sentence, thousands of animals are being eaten alive, many others are running for their lives, whimpering with fear, others are slowly being devoured from within by rasping parasites, thousands of all kinds are dying of starvation, thirst, and disease. It must be so. If there ever is a time of plenty, this very fact will automatically lead to an increase in the population until the natural state of starvation and misery is restored. In a universe of electrons and selfish genes, blind physical forces and genetic replication, some people are going to get hurt, other people are going to get lucky, and you won't find any rhyme or reason in it, nor any justice. The universe that we observe has precisely the properties we should expect if there is, at bottom, no design, no purpose, no evil, no*

good, nothing but pitiless indifference.
Richard Dawkins, *River Out of Eden: A Darwinian View of Life* (Basic Books, 1996) pp131-132

It is not the concern of this chapter to provide a rebuttal of Dawkins. Scientist-theologians such as Alistair McGrath have made comprehensive responses and are worth reading by those interested in the philosophical and scientific issues. The point I wish to make is that in the midst of the ambiguity of life, where we see pain and joy, cruelty and beauty, hatred and love, Jesus brings us a vision of the universe as inhabited by a gracious, loving God, who longs for us and invests our lives with purpose. When we surrender ourselves to the love of God for us and all creation, when we allow it to wash over us and fill our senses, we find layers of meaning and purpose that suffering cannot destroy.

Moreover, there is a sense in which suffering provides opportunities for the good life. In becoming human and making himself vulnerable to suffering, Jesus afforded others the opportunity to extend love to him. The Gospels tell of a group of women, for example, who provided for Jesus financially, who stood by him to the end, and who cared for his body after he had died. It was his weakness and suffering that gave those women the opportunity to experience their humanity in a deep and profound way.

One of the greatest illusions of contemporary life is that we are self-made people and to see need of others as diminishing our humanity. The truth is quite the reverse. We are created to need one another. This is something my progressing Parkinson's has taught me. I cannot get by without assistance from others, whether it be Sandy buttoning up my shirtsleeves, a friend cutting up my food, or a complete stranger offering to help me carry something. I initially found this embarrassing and humiliating, but I have since come to realise that in humbling myself to accept help from others I'm actually experiencing grace and love in ways I had never known before. Rather than seeing this as an imposition upon others I now see it is an opportunity for them to exercise their humanity. It should not take suffering to do this, but caring for each other at our points of weakness, disability and pain makes both the giver and the receiver of care more human.

Living Hopefully Through Suffering

Crucifixion was not the end of the Jesus story. After the crucifixion came the resurrection. Jesus was raised from the dead to a new existence where he was free from disease, decay and death. And this was not to be a unique experience belonging only to Christ. His resurrection was, like his miracles, a sign of what is to come for all of us.

> *Christ has been raised from the dead, the first fruits of those who have died. For since death came through a human being, the resurrection of the dead has also come through a human being; for as all die in Adam, so all will be made alive in Christ. But each in his own order: Christ the first fruits, then at his coming those who belong to Christ. Then comes the end, when he hands over the kingdom to God the Father, after he has destroyed every ruler and every authority and power. For he must reign until he has put all his enemies under his feet. The last enemy to be destroyed is death.*
> 1 Corinthians 15:20-26 NRSV

According to the Old Testament, a time was coming when God would set the world right. The dead would be raised to life and a new age would begin in which all that mars life was removed. That resurrection occurred to Jesus signaled that the new era had begun. Christ's resurrection was the "firstfruits", a reference to the first fruit harvested each season and dedicated to God in gratitude for the harvest to come. In the same way, Christ's resurrection is the sign of the resurrection of all that is to come at the time of his return. It's at this time, said Paul, that all the enemies of humankind will be defeated – violence, hunger, greed, decay and death itself.

The Bible shows little interest in explaining the origins of evil. Its interest is rather in the destruction of evil, something secured by the resurrection of Jesus. It doesn't offer me an explanation of why I suffer nor does it seek to defend God. What it offers me is hope.

We may suffer in the present, but a time is coming when the world will be made new and there will be no more mourning or crying or pain. I have found this a source of great hope as my body continues stubbornly in its rebellion against the dictates of my mind. There are difficult years in front of me, but those few years will be followed by an eternity in which I will have a body more glorious than I can imagine. Does this lesson the suffering I will experience? No it does not. But it does contextualise my suffering and gives me hope.

Living with Jesus through Suffering

If the resurrection is the promise of a transformed future, it is also the promise of divine presence. In Matthew's account of Jesus's life the final word is left to Jesus.

Surely I will be with you always, to the very end of the age.

When Jesus uttered these words it was in the knowledge that just as he had suffered in going about God's mission, so too would his disciples, some even to the point of being executed by crucifixion.

Ironically he begins his final words by declaring that "all authority in heaven and on earth has been given to me". This no doubt led his followers to wonder if he would now bring about the end of the age and the complete inauguration of God's reign of justice, healing and joy. But no, that is yet to come. In the meantime Jesus uses his authority to cast a vision of who we and our world can be, to gently call us to that way, and to offer us welcome, grace, forgiveness, hope as we journey along that path. Perhaps greater than all these he offers us his presence, the knowledge that whatever we pass through he is present with us, feeling our pain and woundedness, whispering hope into our hearts and assuring us that we are never alone and never beyond the reach of God's love.

Suffering Like Jesus

Jesus then provides the lens through which Christians ought to view suffering. This means that we accept suffering as part and parcel of life. Attempts to deny or evade this simply prevent us from coming to grips with reality. Perhaps the worst example of this I have experienced came when I was invited to pray for the dying father of a member of my congregation. As I entered the hospital room in which he lay unconscious and just hours from death it was my intention to offer a short prayer asking God to comfort those who were grieving and to quietly exit, leaving the family to say their final goodbyes. I was introduced to other members of the family and the pastor of the church a number of them attended. They began to pray and it soon became evident that their idea of appropriate prayer was different to mine. They prayed fervently and at great length for God to heal their father, even now at this late stage to raise him up to life, and they would accept no other outcome. Their father was not healed and their refusal to accept his imminent death prevented them from making a good farewell and from finding comfort in

God.

This does not mean we resign ourselves to suffering. There will be times when our healing comes in full this side of resurrection, times when it comes in part, and times when all healing awaits the resurrection. For all of us a time will come when we need to accept the inevitability of suffering and death. But we will never forget that it is not "natural". It is an enemy to be defeated, an unwelcome intrusion into God's good world. We accept its reality but refuse to treat it as the ultimate reality. Rather, we join the way of Jesus and pursue his reign, which will be ultimate, in our lives and world. Where injustice exists we will fight it; where relationships have broken down we will seek reconciliation and forgiveness; where disease wracks bodies we will apply ourselves to finding cures; where poverty occurs we will share our resources; where people are struggling, wounded, or despairing, we will be present and caring.

And we do this inspired by the hope that suffering will not be the last word in the human experience, that a day is coming when the deepest wounds will be healed, bodies paralysed by vicious diseases will run freely through open fields, tortured minds will be lucid, depression will give way to unadulterated joy, war will give way to peace, hatred will give way to love, and it finally will be on earth as it is in heaven.

Questions for Reflection

1. In what ways have pain and suffering touched your life? How has this shaped you?

2. We all need a narrative, a story about the world, that helps us make our way through suffering. What stories do people in our culture tell to explain suffering? A Christian approach calls for

imagination, a willingness to see that life is more than what we presently see, touch and experience. It is to allow the life, death, resurrection and return of Jesus to shape our understanding of life and our response to it. In what ways does the Jesus story help you make sense of suffering?

3. Jesus modelled the way to respond to suffering. Identify one thing from your reading that you will build into your life.

A Prayer

Jesus,
You did not come to our world meeting violence with violence,
hatred with hatred, or force with force.

Rather, you met violence by turning the other cheek,
hatred with love, force with hope.

And so you became the wounded healer, the crucified lover, the servant leader.

We are grieved that the world you crafted with such care and joy has become home to suffering,
to fear, pain, despair, and dread.

Grant us the courage to face the suffering before us,
the wisdom to find meaning amidst the chaos,
the hope that reminds us a better world is coming,
and the faith that reassures us you are near.

Chapter Two

Hagar. God Sees Me

In the late 1960's an old woman was a patient in the Ashludie Hospital in Dundee, Scotland. After she died a poem was found among her belongings. She had copied it by hand from a magazine.

What do you see, nurses what do you see
What are you thinking when you are looking at me
A crabbit old woman, not very wise,
Uncertain of habit, with faraway eyes,
Who dribbles her food and makes no reply
When you say in a loud voice - I do wish you'd try
Who seems not to notice the things that you do
And forever is losing a stocking or shoe,
Who unresisting or not, lets you do as you will
With bathing and feeding, the long day to fill
Is that what you are thinking, is that what you see,
Then open your eyes, nurses, you're not looking at me.

I'll tell you who I am as I sit here so still,
As I am used at your bidding, as I eat at your will,
I am a small child of ten with a father and mother,
Brothers and sisters who love one another,
A young girl of 16 with wings on her feet
Dreaming that soon now a lover she'll meet;

A bride at 20 - my heart gives a leap,
Remembering the vows that I promised to keep
At 25 now I have young of my own
Who need me to build a secure, happy home;
A woman of 30 my young now grow fast,
Bound to each other with ties that should last,
At 40 my young sons have grown and are gone;
But my man's beside me to see I don't mourn;
At 50, once more babies play around my knee.
Again we know children, my loved one and me
Dark days are upon me, my husband is dead,
I look at the future, I shudder with dread,
For my young are all rearing young of their own
And I think of the years and the love that I've known.

I'm an old woman now and nature is cruel
'tis her jest to make old age look like a fool.
The body it crumbles, grace and vigour depart,
There is now a stone where once was a heart
But inside this old carcass a young girl still dwells
And now and again my battered heart swells
I remember the joys I remember the pain,
And I'm loving and living life over again.
I think of the years all too few - gone too fast,
And accept the stark fact that nothing can last.

So open your eyes, nurses open and see
Not a crabbit old woman
Look closer - see me.

One of the greatest fears to assail the human heart is that we will be alone, unwanted, unnoticed, unloved. We want to know that we matter. That we are seen.

For people of faith there is an added dimension to this. We want to know that we are seen by God. Yet when we suffer God often seems distant. CS Lewis wrote one of the most influential books on God and suffering, yet when his wife died of cancer he found God to be spectacularly absent. In *A Grief Observed* he wrote

> *Meanwhile, where is God? This is one of the most disquieting symptoms. When you are happy, so happy that you have no sense of needing Him, so happy that you are tempted to feel His claims upon you as an interruption, if you remember yourself and turn to Him with gratitude and praise, you will be—or so it feels—welcomed with open arms. But go to Him when your need is desperate, when all other help is vain, and what do you find? A door slammed in your face, and a sound of bolting and double bolting on the inside. After that, silenc8e. You may as well turn away. The longer you wait, the more emphatic the silence will become.*
> CS Lewis, *A Grief Observed* (Harper-Collins e-books, 1996) pp5-6

It's at times like these that we need the stories of our faith tradition. When everything within our experience screams that God does not see us, our tradition helps us to see an alternate reality, to climb into the stories of those who have gone before us and live off their experiences even as ours betray us. In this chapter we will explore one of these stories, a shocking story of suffering and abuse, that ends with this conclusion

So [Hagar] called the name of the Lord who spoke to her, 'You are El, who sees me'; for she said, 'Truly have I see him who looks after me?'
Genesis 16:13 NRSV

The Life of a Slave

The story of Hagar the slave girl comes to us from the book of Genesis. It revolves around three characters: Sarai; her husband Abram; and her slave girl Hagar.

To understand this story we need to go back to the opening chapters of Genesis, to the story of the creation of the world. It is beautiful, abundant, and blessed. Humankind is created in God's image and commissioned to rule the earth as God's representatives and to multiply and fill it. The story envisages a future in which the earth is filled with people and communities that reflect the love, grace, kindness, goodness, and justice of God, and find their place as creatures who worship their God. We read on in horror as humankind turns against God's call. Rather than worshipping God, human beings strive to be gods themselves. Rather than filling the earth with communities of love and justice, they fill it with communities that are violent, greedy and unjust.

In Genesis chapter 12 God commences a plan to restore blessing to creation. Abram is plucked from obscurity to play a central role in this plan. He will be the father of a great nation that will live under the blessing of God and as other nations see this blessing they too will return to God. This way blessing will return to all peoples on earth.

A serious problem soon emerges. Abram has no heirs and his wife Sarai is infertile. Without a child how will God's promise be fulfilled?

For Sarai this is a matter of great shame, for in the patriarchal culture of the Ancient Near East one of a woman's primary sources of honour was to produce heirs for her husband. Sarai grows desperate and out of that desperation strikes upon a plan. She will use her servant girl Hagar as a substitute. She will send Hagar to the bed of her husband Abram and the child that is produced will belong to Sarai.

Hagar was Sarai's slave. She was purchased. A piece of property. With no control over her life. An object to be used as Sarai chose. This included use for sex. Sarai aimed to "obtain children by her". Because she owned Hagar, any child born to her would be considered Sarai's. So Sarai *gave* Hagar to Abram. Hagar had no say in it. She was a mere tool by which Sarai would obtain children.

As foreign as this sounds to Western ears, it was accepted custom in Sarai's world. This could not, however, erase the reality that Hagar was reduced to the status of sex slave. Nor does the biblical story approve, even though it be set within the patriarchal value system of the Ancient Near East. God had promised Sarai would have her own child but rather than trusting in God Sarai took matters into her own hands. The whole sordid story is described in terms that deliberately echo the fall of Adam and Eve. Just as Eve took the fruit and gave it to her husband, so Sarah took her servant girl and gave her to her husband. Just as Adam listened to the voice of his wife and obeyed her, so Abram listened to the voice of his wife and obeyed her. We don't know how many times Hagar was forced to sleep with the old man Abram, but she eventually conceived.

Hagar flees

When [Hagar] saw that she had conceived, she looked with contempt on her mistress.

Then Sarai said to Abram, 'May the wrong done to me be on you! I gave my slave-girl to your embrace, and when she saw that she had conceived, she looked on me with contempt. May the Lord judge between you and me!' But Abram said to Sarai, 'Your slave-girl is in your power; do to her as you please.' Then Sarai dealt harshly with her, and she ran away from her.
Genesis 16:4-6 NRSV

It is not surprising that Hagar's pregnancy created an intolerable tension between the slave-girl and her mistress. Hagar gave Abram the very thing Sarai could not and Hagar grew arrogant about it. The Biblical text says Hagar looked on her mistress with contempt. Sarai, already shamed by her infertility, felt that shame every time she looked at Hagar's pregnant body. To be shown contempt only made matters worse. Sarai retaliated by doing everything she could to make Hagar's life miserable. She "dealt harshly" with Hagar, the same language used to describe the treatment of the Israelites while enslaved in Egypt.

Abram also acted shamefully. The text says that Sarah gave him Hagar as a wife, which meant Abram should have protected her and recognised her rights as a wife. Instead he treated Hagar as though she never ceased being a slave girl of Sarai and told Sarai to do whatever she pleased to Hagar.

Things became so bad that Hagar ran away. This was a dramatic step. In the patriarchal culture of the Ancient Near East a woman not attached to a male was extremely vulnerable to poverty, hunger, exploitation and abuse. Hagar's situation was desperate. The situation she left and the situation she entered were both awful.

The God Who Sees

The angel of the Lord found her by a spring of water in the wilderness, the spring on the way to Shur. And he said, 'Hagar, slave-girl of Sarai, where have you come from and where are you going?' She said, 'I am running away from my mistress Sarai.' The angel of the Lord said to her, 'Return to your mistress, and submit to her.' The angel of the Lord also said to her, 'I will so greatly multiply your offspring that they cannot be counted for multitude.' ...

So she called the name of the Lord who spoke to her, 'You are El, who sees me'; for she said, 'Truly have I see him who looks after me?' For this reason the well is called 'Well of the Living who sees me'; it lies between Kadesh and Bered.
Genesis 16:7-14 NRSV

It was at this point that God met Hagar. The text says the angel of the Lord, who in the Old Testament represents God, *found* Hagar. It was not Hagar who searched for God, but God who searched out and found Hagar.

Once God found Hagar he did two things. First, God told Hagar to return to Sarai and to submit to her. Given the torment she had experienced at Sarai's hands this was difficult guidance to follow, but the vulnerability of a single, unattached, runaway slave woman in the Ancient Near East likely made it the best of what were only difficult options. In a broken world we sometimes find the best option for us at any given time is far from the ideal.

Second, God created hope. Hagar's situation may have been difficult, but God declared he would bless her with a son and a nation. Indeed, the text suggests that this was the way God "gave heed" to Hagar's difficulties.

The key to making sense of this is to remember Sarai intended to keep Hagar's child as her own. God promised Hagar this would not be the case. She would name her son and through him she would have many descendants. In the historical context this was received as a tremendous blessing. Sarai will not be able to take Hagar's child from her.

Until this point Hagar knew that God saw Abram and Sarai, that God had appeared to them and made promises to them. Now she knew that God saw her too, cared for her too, and had a future for her too. She may be an Egyptian slave girl who was ruthlessly manipulated by her mistress, but she was seen by God.

What Does It Mean to Say God Sees?

Throughout the Bible, God is the one who sees, and particularly the one who sees those in need. When the Israelites were oppressed as slaves in Egypt, God saw them

> *Then the Lord said, 'I have observed the misery of my people who are in Egypt; I have heard their cry on account of their taskmasters. Indeed, I know their sufferings, and I have come down to deliver them from the Egyptians, and to bring them up out of that land to a good and broad land, a land flowing with milk and honey.*
> Exodus 3:7-8 NRSV

Centuries later when the nation once more languished under oppression, the people were tempted to think they had been forgotten by God. But it was not so

> *Zion said, 'The Lord has forsaken me, my Lord has forgotten me.'*

> *Can a woman forget her nursing-child,*
> *or show no compassion for the child of her womb?*
> *Even these may forget,*
> *yet I will not forget you.*
> *See, I have inscribed you on the palms of my hands;*
> *your walls are continually before me.*
> Isaiah 49:14-15 NRSV

When the Bible says that God sees people it means two things. First, it signals that we are the focus of God's attention. No matter how absent God may seem, the reality is God is never absent but holds each one of us in his heart. No matter what our emotions say, the truth is that God is like the mother described in Isaiah 49 who has our names inscribed on her hands and can't be anything other than filled with compassion.

Second, it means that God will act to bring about a resolution of the situation. When God saw Hagar he sent her back to Abraham and Sarai with the promise that her child would be hers and the father of a nation. When God saw Israel enslaved in Egypt, he acted to liberate the people. The New Testament expands the horizons of God's action to see that deliverance from that which causes us to suffer may come not in this life, but in the resurrection from the dead and the creation of a new heavens and earth. Certainly there are occasions God acts to fully and completely deliver us right now, but the more typical pattern is for that final and full deliverance to come in the new age ahead.

This has been true in my experience. Parkinson's and Leukemia are not the first life threatening illnesses I have had. When I was a child I had a heart condition known as cardiomyopathy. At one stage my heart began enlarging at such a rate that complete and irreversible failure was imminent. I was in the care of some of Australia's leading heart specialists and they despaired of any solution. I was placed on medication and in time my heart stopped enlarging, returned to its normal size and now shows no sign of injury. My specialists were amazed. There was nothing in the treatments they administered that in their eyes could explain what had happened.

On my final visit to my specialist, he shook his head and said "Scott, you're a modern medical miracle." I was baffled. Wasn't it the medication he had given me that healed my heart? I'll never forget his answer. "There is nothing in the drug that can explain why your heart has returned to normal. It's just one of those medical miracles." Whether it was a miraculous healing or some unknown natural processes were at play, I believe God saw me and came to my aid. And I believe the same is true as I battle Parkinson's. I do not expect any healing this side of the grave, but my healing will come in the resurrection, for God still sees me.

Being Seen by God Today

Through history many have shared the experience of Hagar and Israel. Martin Luther King was just twenty-six years old when he was appointed leader of the US civil rights campaign in Montgomery, Alabama. Apart from terrifying threats from the Ku Klux Klan, King was harassed by police. Arrested for driving five miles per hour over the speed limit he was given his first stint in jail. The night after his release he was at home when the phone rang. "Nigger", said a menacing voice on the other end, "we are tired of you and your mess now. And if you aren't out of this town in three days, we're going to blow your brains out and blow up your house."

King was unnerved and very afraid – for himself, for his wife and for his little children. Shortly after the phone call he sat at his kitchen table drinking a cup of coffee.

"And I sat at that table" he said, "thinking about that little girl and thinking about the fact that she could be taken away from me at any minute. And I started thinking about a dedicated, devoted and loyal wife, who was over there asleep….And I got to the point where I couldn't take it anymore. I was weak…

And I discovered then that religion had to become real to me, and I had to know God for myself. And I bowed down over that cup of coffee. I will never forget it…I said, 'Lord, I'm down here trying to do what's right. I think I'm right. I think the cause we represent is right. But Lord, I must confess that I'm weak now. I'm faltering. I'm losing my courage….And it seemed to me at that moment that I could hear an inner voice saying to me, 'Martin Luther, stand up for righteousness. Stand up for justice. Stand up for truth. And lo, I will be with you, even until the end of the world.'…I heard the voice of Jesus saying still to fight on. He promised never to leave me, never to leave me alone. No never alone. No never alone. He promised never to leave me, never to leave me alone.

David Garrow, *Bearing The Cross. Martin Luther King Jr And The Southern Christian Leadership Conference* (Vintage, 1986)

Martin Luther King discovered that God saw him.

When I was a youth pastor a young woman started attending our programs. Her parents had Munchausen's syndrome, a terrible psychiatric disorder. Although their daughter was healthy, they were convinced she was ill. For years Elisabeth was confined to her bed, which saw her develop a severe curvature of the spine and wasted muscles. When she came to our youth group Elisabeth could not walk or hold her head up. Nonetheless, Elisabeth possessed a remarkable faith in God. She told me that through all those years of suffering she had a strong sense of God's presence and love. She knew that God saw her and found it tremendously comforting.

Over the months that followed her arrival at youth group Elisabeth came out of herself. She gained a new confidence, regained muscle strength, found friendships, and developed a whole new lease on life. I believe that it was through the youth group that God acted to bring some resolution to her situation, and that while she would never regain full health this side of the resurrection, she was experiencing in part the full and complete restoration that is to come.

Whether your experience is like that of Elisabeth, who was blessed with a strong sense of God's presence, or that of CS Lewis for whom heaven was silent, the stories of our faith tradition remind us that God is present and that whatever life may throw at us God will bring resolution. It may come in small ways or dramatic ways in the present, but it will come fully and completely in the resurrection. For you are not forgotten. God sees you.

Questions for Reflection

1. When and in what circumstances have you been most aware of God's presence? When and in what circumstances have you felt unseen by God?

2. According to Genesis 1 human beings are the image of God on the earth. We make the invisible God visible to one another. In what ways has the love and care of others been for you a signal of God's love and care? How have you been able to be a vehicle of God's love and care to others?

3. Close your eyes and imagine God speaking to you. God calls your name and says "I see you." Listen to these words over and over. What difference does it make to know that God sees you?

A Prayer

Loving God,
You are El, the God who sees me.

How I long to be seen,
to feel your eyes beholding me with compassion,
to know deep in my bones that you gaze on me
with a heart full of love.

I will look for you and listen for you.
Grant me eyes that see and ears that hear.
And so long as the darkness hides you
keep me wrapped up inside the stories of my faith,
until that moment I glimpse your reality
and find comfort in your presence.

Chapter Three

Psalms. The Language of Grief

A few years ago I found myself in S21, a former high school in Phnom Penn, Cambodia, in which the madman Pol Pot tortured thousands of Cambodians. The savagery was incomprehensible to me, and served the insane end of forcing people to confess to crimes they had never committed, after which they were executed.

From S21 I travelled to the "killing fields", beautiful open spaces, surrounded by graceful trees, birdsong, and a brilliant blue sky. Anywhere else in the world this setting would create feelings of peace, but not here. Beneath the ground upon which I walked lay the bones of countless Cambodians who were murdered by Pol Pot and his soldiers. This was a mass grave site. The most haunting moment was coming upon "the killing tree". It was here that soldiers took babies and young children and smashed their heads against the trunk of the tree until they were dead.

It was one of the most harrowing days of my life. I was filled with anger, sadness, despair, and bewilderment. I was angry that people could do this to one another. I was desperately sad for those who had lived through this bloody history. I despaired because I knew this will happen again somewhere else in the world. And I was bewildered that God could let all this happen.

When we suffer, or we encounter the suffering of others, it can be as though the world falls apart. Everything we took for granted can be brought into question. Many find themselves going through a grieving process. First there is denial, then anger, bargaining, sadness, and finally acceptance. At the end of a process like this we find we cannot go back to the simplistic platitudes we perhaps offered in the past.

How do you get through this with your faith intact? How do you find God when you're in the stage of denial or anger or bargaining or sadness? What do you do when the songs you sing at church declare that God is good, that you are so in love with him, that all you want to do is sing his praises, when in fact you're not at all sure that God is good, you're not at all sure that you love and trust him, and you definitely don't want to sing his praises?

To answer that we turn to the Psalms, the prayer book of Israel. Like our songbooks, the psalms contain celebrations of God's goodness, majesty, love and presence. Unlike our songbooks they also contain expressions of doubt, anger, bewilderment, feelings of being abandoned by God and deep questioning of God.

> *How long, Lord? Will you forget me forever?*
> *How long will you hide your face from me?*
> *How long must I wrestle with my thoughts*
> *and day after day have sorrow in my heart?*
> *How long will my enemy triumph over me?*
> Psalm 13:1-2 NRSV

> *My God, my God, why have you forsaken me?*
> *Why are you so far from saving me,*
> *so far from my cries of anguish?*

My God, I cry out by day, but you do not answer,
by night, but I find no rest.
Psalm 22:1-2 NRSV

Listen to my prayer, O God,
do not ignore my plea;
hear me and answer me.
My thoughts trouble me and I am distraught
because of what my enemy is saying,
because of the threats of the wicked;
for they bring down suffering on me
and assail me in their anger.
My heart is in anguish within me;
the terrors of death have fallen on me.
Fear and trembling have beset me;
horror has overwhelmed me.
Psalm 55:1-4 NRSV

Lord, you are the God who saves me;
day and night I cry out to you.
May my prayer come before you;
turn your ear to my cry.
I am overwhelmed with troubles
and my life draws near to death.
I am counted among those who go down to the pit;
I am like one without strength.
I am set apart with the dead,
like the slain who lie in the grave,
whom you remember no more,
who are cut off from your care.
You have put me in the lowest pit,
in the darkest depths.

Your wrath lies heavily on me;
you have overwhelmed me with all your waves.
You have taken from me my closest friends
and have made me repulsive to them.
I am confined and cannot escape;
my eyes are dim with grief....
But I cry to you for help, Lord;
in the morning my prayer comes before you.
Why, Lord, do you reject me
and hide your face from me?
Psalm 88:1-14 NRSV

Prayers of Lament

The German scholar Herman Gunkel identified five main types of psalm:

1. Hymns of Praise and Celebration;
2. Lament or Complaint Psalms;
3. Royal Psalms;
4. Thanksgiving Psalms;
5. Wisdom Psalms.

It is the lament psalms that are the focus of our attention, for they are filled with doubt, questioning, complaint and even anger towards God. These prayers drip with emotion. The psalm writer is in pain and pours it all out to God. In *The Spirituality of the Psalms* Walter Bruggemann describes these as psalms of disorientation. The settled, ordered world the psalmist once knew - where the sun shone brightly, relationships were rewarding, and God was seen to pour out blessings - collapses and chaos and confusion seem to reign.

In some of these laments the psalmist expresses raw and unrestrained feelings of vengeance. Psalm 137 was written by an

Israelite who had lived through an invasion and been carried off to live in exile another land. The psalmist remembers the gloating of the enemy as the city was torn to the ground, the screams of pain as limbs were severed from bodies, the sexual assaults and the wanton destruction of things he held dear. The psalm is seething with bitterness and anger:

> *"Happy are those who repay you according to what you have done to us. Happy are those who seize your infants and dash them against the rocks."*

This is not the "Father forgive them" moment that Jesus modelled for us from the cross; this is not love for your enemy; this is pure, visceral hatred. Yet here it is in the prayer book of Israel. It is not there to teach us that such feelings are good, but to show that such feelings are real, that we should not suppress them, but own them and pour them out to our God.

We are sometimes prevented from such brutal honesty out of fear God is brittle and easily offended. This was true of me when I was a teenager. I understood that God was so repulsed by sin that he could not bear to be in its presence and was filled with righteous indignation and pure anger against sinners. To pour out bitter speech, fantasies of revenge, feelings of doubt, would surely court the displeasure of God? The lament psalms teach us that this is not the case. God is not brittle, nor is God easily offended. This is the God who was incarnate in Christ, who didn't recoil at the sinners around him but offered them friendship, embrace and welcome, sat down at table and ate, drank, conversed and laughed with them.

The Shape of Lament

But anguish and complaint are not the totality of the lament psalms. They tend to follow a pattern. The psalm writer begins with complaint but then moves to a plea for God to act, and finishes often, but not always, with an expression of certainty that God will respond. This conviction is not wishful thinking but comes about as the writer remembers the ways God acted in the past, both the past of personal experience and the past of the nation. The psalmist may not understand why God appears silent, but can be confident that the silence will be broken, for God has always proven faithful in the past.

Psalm 22, for example, begins with the agonising cry "My God, my God, why have you forsaken me?" The writer feels completely abandoned by God. As the text progresses it becomes clear that the psalm writer is physically very weak and subject to derision and mocking from those around him. The description would fit the situation of a person who suffers an illness that invoked disgust and rejection. Likewise, it would fit the circumstances of a leader captured by his enemies. Whatever the circumstance, in the midst of his despair the psalm writer calls out to God and is distressed to find God meets the prayer with silence.

Importantly, the psalmist doesn't stay there. In the midst of the pain is the memory of how God acted for the people in the past (verses 3-8) and how God was experienced during the psalmist's childhood (verses 9-11). This emboldens the writer, providing cause to believe that God will prove dependable again.

The mood changes dramatically in the second half of the psalm. The psalm writer moves from despair to praise, celebrating the way God delivered him. It's almost as if there is a time gap between the first half of the psalm and the second half, with God having acted to redeem the psalm writer in the space between the first and second parts.

The movement from the pain of the present, to remembering the action of God in the past, and from there having hope for the future is critically important. It is this way that prayer becomes an opportunity to move forward.

Lament is not a rejection of God and faith in the light of bitter and painful experience. It is rather an engaging with God in which we are brutally honest about how we feel and how we see things. To this we bring the memory of the people of God and our own past experiences, allowing those memories to inform our outlook. This builds confidence that God is near, feels deeply for us and will act.

Lament is an invitation to be honest with God, even when the space we are in is not a good one. Our God is not offended by our doubts, our fears, our disappointment with him, our anger. And it is an invitation to bring the resources of our faith to our questions, anger and doubt, to remember that history has a horizon beyond anything we are experiencing at the moment and to frame our present in light of that larger horizon.

Lament, Christ and Hope

One of the unresolved tensions within the psalms of lament is that the hope of the writer is invariably for God to resolve the situation within the plane of his or her lifetime. Such hope can easily disappoint. There was no rescue for the Cambodians murdered by Pol Pot. Absent a miracle, there will be no healing of my body this side of death.

The corrective is the resurrection of Jesus. This expands our horizon beyond death. It reminds us that God will create a new world, where there is no more suffering, death, crying, mourning or pain. When we remember God's work in the past, we remember the resurrection of Jesus. And on the basis of this work we have confidence that we too will be raised.

Learning to Lament Today

The art of lament has largely disappeared from western Christianity. Our communal worship is filled with songs that express nothing but absolute confidence in the goodness and greatness of God, a celebration of the ways God is present to us. And certainly the psalms are full of such songs. But they are also full of lament. In both private and public worship there was a willingness to make space for both.

We need to do the same. We need to remember that while lamenting moves from despair to resolution and praise, it may take quite a period of time for us to make such a movement in real life. Psalm 137, which we noted earlier, never moves out of despair and anger. There may be times for those who suffer when this is all they can manage. The lament psalms assure them that it's okay to be where they're at, that it's as okay for them to be angry, disheartened, broken-hearted, bewildered and confused as it is to be at peace, filled with faith, and confident about God's presence. God is not offended by our pain, disappointed by our conflicted emotions, nor damaged by our anger.

To our pain we eventually need to bring milestones, both our collective memories of God's presence in the life, death and resurrection of Jesus and our personal memories of points at which God was very real to us.

One of my milestones occurred when I was in my early twenties. Fresh out of theological college I went through a period of intense doubt about the existence of God. I was in the habit of taking late night walks around our neighbourhood and on one of these walks, as I poured out my pain to a God I was not sure I believed in, I was filled with an overwhelming sense that God was present. I cannot explain this. There was nothing particularly spectacular about it, no flashing lights or angelic appearances, just an overwhelming feeling that I have not had before or since. This is for me one of the milestones to which I return to buttress my faith.

These milestones form the rungs of the ladder that will lead us up out of the abyss of despair. To our tortured emotions they whisper gently that God is with us, behind us, beneath us, above us and before us. Above all that God is for us.

Questions for Reflection

1. The psalms of lament assure us that we can pour out our anger, bitterness and pain to God. How do you feel about this? How does lament help you negotiate pain and suffering?

2. Anger, despair, and doubt are all part of the experience of life. But it is unhelpful to get stuck permanently in these. Lament calls us to remember the times we have been aware of God's love and presence and to draw hope from them. What are the milestone experiences of God's love and presence that you draw upon?

3. Create a group lament. Take a situation of pain and suffering. This could be the pain someone in your group is currently experiencing or a situation of pain and suffering in the world. Write down words that express your feeling of pain and confusion about this. Spend some time reading them together in prayer (eg "God, we are angry"). Now spend time identifying milestones that help build your confidence that God will act .

Write them down and then pray them (eg "God we remember that…"). Finally, reflect on how these milestones will impact your living. Write them down and then pray them (eg "God, I will hold onto to your promise.")

A Prayer

God of the angry, the broken-hearted, and the disappointed
Why is it that just when I need you the most
You are spectacularly absent?

I pour my heart out to you day-in-day-out
I long for the tiniest glimpse of your presence,
The merest hint of a word of comfort.
But all I hear is silence. All I see is the dark.

Yet through all the silence, questions and doubts
I remember there have been times in my life when you were as real
to me as the sun, as close to me as the air I breathe,
almost tangible.

I remember that you have been real in the stories of others,
the lepers Jesus healed,
the disturbed that Jesus exorcised,
the broken whom Jesus welcomed.

I feel like Jesus, hanging forlorn on the cross and crying
"My god, my God, why have you forsaken me."

I will remember that following the cross comes resurrection.
However long I wade in these waters of difficulty,
help me to keep my eyes fixed on the resurrection
and to hope in you, the lifegiver.

Chapter Four

Job. The Limits of Wisdom

In the mid 1800's Horatio Spafford, a wealthy and devout Christian and successful lawyer, lived in Chicago with his wife Anna and their five children. The family was active in the abolitionist (antislavery) movement and the spiritual life of their church. But over the course of four years, 1870-1873, their world came crashing down. In 1870 Horatio and Anna were devastated when their youngest child and only son died of scarlet fever. A year later the Great Chicago Fire broke out and Horatio literally watched the bulk of his wealth go up in smoke. Two years later the family set sail for a holiday in Europe. At the last minute Horatio stayed behind to attend to some urgent business. He would follow on a later ship. Anna alone made it to Europe. The ship she and the girls were aboard sank during the crossing and Anna alone survived.

Throughout it all Horatio maintained his faith in God. As he sailed to England to meet Anna, he passed over the place his daughters drowned and penned a famous hymn.

When peace, like a river, attendeth my way,
When sorrows like sea billows roll;

> *Whatever my lot, Thou has taught me to say,*
> *It is well, it is well, with my soul.*

Horatio Spafford's faith was both remarkable and inspirational. Yet not many of us are as reconciled to our suffering as he was. When confronted with suffering we frequently question God's governance of the universe, wondering if God really is all loving or all good or all powerful. Surely he wouldn't allow these things to have happened to us, yet they did. Unable to blame God some will assume they are to blame for the suffering they experience. Perhaps I have neglected God's way and this is sent to bring me to repentance?

These questions are not new. They were asked thousands of years ago in the Old Testament book of Job.

Approaching the book of Job

The book of Job is a product of what Bible scholars refer to as the "wisdom movement" of the Ancient Near East. Members of the wisdom movement believed that there was physical and moral order to the universe and that by discerning that order it was possible to identify principles for successful living. Where priests turned to the Law and prophets received a revelation, the wisdom movement used thoughtful observation to uncover the patterns of life.

These patterns were articulated in short sayings that covered all kinds of life situations, from winning favour with the king to producing good crops.

> *"Plans fail for lack of counsel, but with many advisers they succeed."* 15:22 NRSV

> *"The perverse stir up dissension, and gossips separate close friends"* 16:28 NRSV

"The righteous choose their friends carefully, but the way of the wicked leads them astray." 12:26 NRSV

The danger for the wisdom movement was that in uncovering some order within the universe, it would assume that it had uncovered all the order in the universe. The books of Job and Ecclesiastes represent a corrective to this. In these books we are reminded that life does not always reward the good and penalize the bad, and that reality is far more complex than our minds can fathom.

Job Loses Everything

In order to make its point, the book of Job crafts a fictional account about an impeccably good man who, like Horatio Spafford, lost everything. Job is described as one of the richest men of his era. He had seven thousand sheep, three thousand camels, five hundred bullock and five hundred donkeys. And he was good. Right at the outset we are reminded that he was "blameless and upright, one who feared God and turned away from evil." (1:1) He was exemplary in character; generous with his wealth; protected and assisted the vulnerable; was faithful to his wife; and in all he did sought to honour his Creator.

Then one day he lost everything.

> *One day when his sons and daughters were eating and drinking wine in the eldest brother's house, a messenger came to Job and said, 'The oxen were ploughing and the donkeys were feeding beside them, and the Sabeans fell on them and carried them off, and killed the servants with the edge of the sword; I alone have escaped to tell you.' While he was still speaking, another came and said, 'The fire of God fell from heaven and burned up the*

> *sheep and the servants, and consumed them; I alone have escaped to tell you.' While he was still speaking, another came and said, 'The Chaldeans formed three columns, made a raid on the camels and carried them off, and killed the servants with the edge of the sword; I alone have escaped to tell you.' While he was still speaking, another came and said, 'Your sons and daughters were eating and drinking wine in their eldest brother's house, and suddenly a great wind came across the desert, struck the four corners of the house, and it fell on the young people, and they are dead; I alone have escaped to tell you.'*
>
> Job 1:13-18 NRSV

Soon after Job also loses his health. His body becomes covered in "loathsome sores" (Job 2:7). The man who was once a prosperous, generous, and respected leader in his community lost everything that mattered to him: his children; his wealth; his health; and his reputation. He has gone from one extreme to another, setting up the question that the book tries to answer: what is God doing?

The Reader's View

Throughout the book Job and his friends debate the cause of his suffering. His friends will argue that God is punishing him for some terrible wrong he must have committed. Job will protest his innocence and demand that God answer for treating him unfairly. We, the readers, know that both are wrong, for we have been privy to an exchange between God and Satan during a gathering of God and the angels. One, known as The Accuser, suggests that the only reason Job worships God is to keep the good things God has given him. Take these away and Job will soon turn his back on God.

The Accuser makes the claim that no-one is really righteous, that life consists of a bargain in which human beings do what God desires not because it is good but in order to find God's blessing. God agrees to test the claim and grants Satan the power to strip Job of everything but his life.

It is helpful to remember that Job is a work of faithful fiction, akin to one of Jesus' parables. The scene between God and Satan is not intended to show us how God operates in real life. It is rather, a literary device to let us, the readers, know that Job isare bnot being punished for his sin.

Job and his Wife

Embittered by what occurred, Job's wife urges her husband to curse God and die. Job will have none of this.

> *Naked I came from my mother's womb, and naked I will depart. The Lord gave and the Lord has taken away; may the name of the Lord be praised.*
> Job 1:21 NRSV

Job notes that for years they had enjoyed good things from the hand of God, and so should they not receive bad things in the same fashion? He understands that everything that occurs in his life comes from the hand of God and he is happy to submit to that.

This section of the story concludes by noting that God's confidence in Job was well founded. Despite losing everything he values, Job does not curse God.

The Debate Between Job & His Friends

Job is visited by three friends, who at first do everything right.

> *Now when Job's three friends heard of all these troubles that had come upon him, each of them set out from his home—*

> *Eliphaz the Temanite, Bildad the Shuhite, and Zophar the Naamathite. They met together to go and console and comfort him. When they saw him from a distance, they did not recognize him, and they raised their voices and wept aloud; they tore their robes and threw dust in the air upon their heads. They sat with him on the ground for seven days and seven nights, and no one spoke a word to him, for they saw that his suffering was very great.*
>
> Job 3:11-13 NRSV

Job's friends display enormous empathy. Good friends that they are, they just sit with him, offering the only gift they have, their presence.

After seven days pass the friends decide it's time to speak. As much as they feel for their companion and want to console him, the time has come when they believe they must confront Job. In their opinion, there can be but one reason for the fate that has befallen him – God is punishing Job for some terrible evil he has committed.

In speech after speech they harangue their friend with what appears to them unassailable logic: The universe operates according to the principle of retribution. God rewards the righteous with the good things of the earth and punishes the unrighteous by stripping them of these goods. The only reasonable conclusion is that Job is being punished and his salvation lies in admitting this, after which God will surely restore him. This, for example, is what Eliphaz counsels in chapter 22

> *Is it for your piety that he reproves you,*
> *and enters into judgement with you?*
> *Is not your wickedness great?*
> *There is no end to your iniquities...*

> *Agree with God, and be at peace;*
> *in this way good will come to you.*
> *Receive instruction from his mouth,*
> *and lay up his words in your heart.*
> *If you return to the Almighty, you will be restored.*
> Job 22 NRSV

Job shares their sense that all things come from the hand of God, but not their conclusion. It is not his actions that are unrighteous but God's. The humble acceptance of whatever comes from the hand of God that marked his initial response to the crisis gives way to indignation. God is unfairly and mercilessly pursuing him, driving him to hopelessness and despair. Job demands that God appear and answer for what he is doing.

> *I loathe my life;*
> *I will give free utterance to my complaint;*
> *I will speak in the bitterness of my soul.*
> *I will say to God, Do not condemn me;*
> *let me know why you contend against me.*
> *Does it seem good to you to oppress,*
> *to despise the work of your hands*
> *and favour the schemes of the wicked?*
> *Do you have eyes of flesh?*
> *Do you see as humans see?*
> *Are your days like the days of mortals,*
> *or your years like human years,*
> *that you seek out my iniquity*
> *and search for my sin,*
> *although you know that I am not guilty,*
> *and there is no one to deliver out of your hand?*
> *...Why did you bring me forth from the womb?*

> *Would that I had died before any eye had seen me,*
> *and were as though I had not been,*
> *carried from the womb to the grave.*
> *Are not the days of my life few?*
> *Let me alone, that I may find a little comfort*
> *before I go, never to return,*
> *to the land of gloom and deep darkness,*
> *the land of gloom and chaos,*
> *where light is like darkness.*
> Job 10 NRSV

Chapter after chapter pits Job and his friends against each other and Job against God. The friends seek to defend the honour of God and their attack on Job becomes ever more strident and exasperated. They are astonished at his hard and unrepentant attitude.

Job on the other hand clings stubbornly to his innocence, and in a state of depression, anger and indignation, demands that a capricious God appear and answer for his cruelty.

Elihu

We reach the final chapters of the book and nothing is resolved. A fourth person, the younger man Elihu, enters the debate at chapter 32.

> *Elihu son of Barakel the Buzite, of the family of Ram, became very angry with Job for justifying himself rather than God. He was also angry with the three friends, because they had found no way to refute Job, and yet had condemned him.*
> Job 32:1-3 NRSV

Elihu's role is debated by commentators. Yet whatever role he is intended to play, Elihu no more resolves the issue than Job's three friends. He faults Job for questioning the justice and goodness of God, who punishes the wicked and the proud. Like Job's friends, Elihu is convinced that Job is being punished for his wickedness.

> *Far be it from God to do evil, for the Almighty to do wrong.*
> *He repays everyone for what they have done;*
> *He brings on them what their conduct deserves.*
> *It is unthinkable that God would do wrong.*
> Job 34:10-12 NRSV

A Resolution of Sorts

The tension that builds throughout the book is relieved when God finally appears. God doesn't answer for his actions as Job demanded, nor does God reveal to Job the reasons for his suffering. At the end of the book Job and his friends remain as ignorant of what we the readers know as they were at the start.

When God appears it is not to answer to Job but to challenge him. In these final chapters God asks Job whether he has the wisdom to govern the world.

> *Then the Lord spoke to Job out of the storm. He said:*

> *"Who is this that obscures my plans*
> *with words without knowledge?*
> *Brace yourself like a man;*
> *I will question you,*
> *and you shall answer me.*

> *"Where were you when I laid the earth's foundation?*
> *Tell me, if you understand.*
> *Who marked off its dimensions? Surely you know!*
> *Who stretched a measuring line across it?*

On what were its footings set,
or who laid its cornerstone—
while the morning stars sang together
and all the angels shouted for joy?

"Who shut up the sea behind doors
when it burst forth from the womb,
when I made the clouds its garment
and wrapped it in thick darkness,
when I fixed limits for it
and set its doors and bars in place,
when I said, 'This far you may come and no farther;
here is where your proud waves halt'?

"Have you ever given orders to the morning,
or shown the dawn its place,
that it might take the earth by the edges
and shake the wicked out of it?
The earth takes shape like clay under a seal;
its features stand out like those of a garment.
The wicked are denied their light,
and their upraised arm is broken.
Job 38:1-10 NRSV

God provides case after case of things that happen in the universe over which Job has either no knowledge or no control. It was God, not Job, who called the universe into being, set boundaries for the seas, sends sunshine and rain, imbued the animals with their unique characteristics, provides them with food and watches over them as they give birth, and alone has the power to command the behemoth and leviathan. Job is badly mistaken when he accuses God of being reckless, unjust and cruel. He may not understand God's governing but this should not be taken to mean God is not governing. In short,

God's speech suggests Job doesn't know what he's talking about.

Nor did Job's three friends. God castigates them "for you have not spoken of me what is right". If Job was wrong to argue that God was unjust, they were even more mistaken when they insisted that God governs the universe by the principle of retributive justice. In their attempt to defend the honour of God they defamed God. Their theology was too narrow. They needed to come to grips with the fact that they lived in a universe where the righteous sometimes suffered and the wicked sometimes prospered.

The world it seems, is a much more complex place than either Job or his friends allowed. Justice, understood as the retribution and reward principle, does operate at some scale, but it cannot account for everything that happens. Other factors are at play, and God alone has the capacity and wisdom to know them and order the world wisely.

The Way of Wisdom

How do we live in a universe like this? The book's answer is provided in chapter 28, which most commentators see as an interlude before Job's final speech. The chapter asks where wisdom, the knowledge of how to live successfully, can be found. The writer insists that is beyond the capacity of humans to discover wisdom for themselves.

> *It is hidden from the eyes of every living thing…*
> *God understands the way to it [wisdom]*
> *And he alone knows where it dwells*
> *for he views the ends of the earth*
> *and sees everything under the heavens…*
> *And he said to the human race,*

> *'The fear of the Lord – that is wisdom,*
> *and to shun evil is understanding.'*
> Job 28:23,28 NRSV

There is wisdom that is beyond our capacity to read off the circumstances of life. Things happen in our lives and our world that we struggle to make sense of. Why did my friend's child die? Why did God miraculously heal my father of his addiction to nicotine, yet is impervious to the pleas of other nicotine addicts? Why do I have Parkinson's? Why does God not alleviate poverty and prevent war? For centuries philosophers and theologians have sought to answer such questions, but even the most logically coherent of their solutions seem cold.

The story of Job calls us to face suffering with humility and trust. We need the humility to recognise that there is much about God and the world that we don't know and may never know, and at the same time to trust in the God we do know. Chapter 28 describes this as "fearing the Lord". This is the first time in Job that the title "the Lord" is used of God, marking a shift from a generic reference to God to a term that calls to mind Israel's unique name for God, "the Lord" (Yahweh). This is the name by which God revealed himself to Israel and gave them his Law, highlighting that for the Israelite wisdom movement, the starting point for all reflection was service of the God of their past, present and future. Our attempts to read order off creation may fail but we can cling to the God who revealed himself in Jesus.

The Restoration

The story ends with God restoring to Job everything he had lost. Indeed "the Lord gave Job twice as much as he had before" (42:10). The book concludes

> *After this Job lived for one hundred and forty years, and saw his children and his children's children, four generations. And Job died, old and full of days.*
> JOB 42:16 NRSV

This reminds us that while God's ways may be unfathomable, they are not chaotic. The message of Job is not that the universe is disordered but that it is often beyond our capacity to understand how God orders it. Yet precisely because God is good, in the end God will ensure good prevails. As we have already noted in preceding chapters, the horizons for justice may well lie beyond this age, but justice and healing will eventually prevail.

Living it Out

The central insight of the wisdom movement, that the world has an inbuilt moral order, is important. Our actions have predictable consequences. If I get behind the wheel of my car while drunk, my actions are directly responsible for the accident that I may have. If I ignore medical advice about my diet, I may well end up with diet induced diabetes. On the flip side, the order in the universe enables us to construct lives that are meaningful. Imagine trying to live if the sun rose at random and unpredictable hours or if the laws of physics turned in on themselves on an ad hoc basis.

To this we must add the insights of story of Job, that at times things don't go to plan and we can find ourselves stuck in an abyss of uncertainty and despair. Rarely is there any direct relation between our suffering and our sin. More often than not it is a result of the actions of others or simply from living in a world where earthquakes occur, tree branches fall, and cancerous cells divide. We must avoid a simplistic view of God that sees his punishing hand behind these events.

This not only relieves us of blaming ourselves for our suffering, but relieves us of viewing God as a monster. It is not uncommon for people to reject God on the basis that they refuse to worship a God who causes children to suffer cancer, who refuses to stop wars, and who inflicts untold suffering on the world's poor. The assumption is that the universe should operate on the principle of retributive justice, that good things should happen to good people and bad things to bad people. The story of Job insists that it does not, but that it is governed by a good God whose ways are often mysterious.

After the Second World War came to a close, some graffiti was found in a cellar that had been used to hide Jews from the Nazis. One suspects the author was familiar with Job's story. The graffiti read

I believe in the sun
even when it isn't shining.
I believe in love
even when I am alone.
I believe in God
even when he is silent.

Questions for Reflection

1. Suffering raises painful questions about God's governance of the universe. What question about God and God's ways does your own suffering and that of others raise for you??

2. Rather than explaining God's actions, the book of Job calls us to recognise that the universe is incredibly complex. We cannot reduce reality to simple binaries such as "if God is just then the

good must always be rewarded and the evil punished". Rather, Job suggests we must humbly accept our limitations and trust God's wisdom. How helpful do you find this perspective? What are the advantages of trusting God? What are the challenges?

3. We live in an era in which knowledge is king. If we can't know it, we can't be sure of it. What things help you trust in God even when you don't understand what God is doing?

A Prayer

God, I want explanations.
Explanations for what has happened to me.
Explanations for what happens to others.
I want to understand how life is ordered.

But you don't give me explanations.
You give me yourself

And call me to trust your wisdom even as mine fails
And to hope in the future you are creating even when I cannot see it.

It's a bold and audacious ask,
but one to which I say "yes".

Chapter Five

Qoholet. Enjoy the Sunshine While You Can

Ecclesiastes is one of the strangest books in the Bible, for it repeats over and over two themes that appear to be completely at odds with biblical faith. The first and most well-known is the cry that "Meaningless! Meaningless! Everything is meaningless!" The author, a teacher called Qoholet, set himself the task of examining the great pursuits of humankind - amassing wealth, gaining knowledge, undertaking building projects, experiencing pleasure - yet concluded that whatever he pursued was meaningless.

Equally disorienting is the second refrain of the book, the commendation to seek pleasure and enjoyment in life. "I know that there is nothing better for them [people] than to be happy and enjoy themselves as long as they live" the author writes (3:12). Faced with the meaninglessness of life, the book suggests that we take the opportunity to soak up every pleasurable moment that we can. This sounds like it has more in common with the "eat, drink and be merry, for tomorrow we may die" attitude of hedonism than faith!

In the writings of Qoholet we find unique insight into how we can live when life doesn't turn out the way we hoped. More than any other book in the Bible, Ecclesiastes comes face-to-face with the apparent absurdity of suffering, yet in the midst of the uncertainties that surround life encourages us to soak up and enjoy those delectable moments that come our way.

The Wrong Way to Read Ecclesiastes

Ecclesiastes is sometimes read as though Qoholet was contrasting two world views, a secular world view which strives to find meaning in things other than God, and a faith-filled approach which seeks to live God's way. On this view the cry that "meaningless, meaningless, everything is meaningless" represents the book's evaluation of a godless life. The positive statements by contrast represent the way of faith.

As neat as it sounds, this reading is not convincing, for the "positive" and "negative" arguments sit side by side and are presented as the teaching of Qoholet. When Qoholet declares that life is meaningless he is articulating the conclusion he has reached as a person of faith. When he encourages us to enjoy the good things of life it is a genuine encouragement. Qoholet seems to be arguing that life's pursuits can be meaningless *and* that we should enjoy what we can *and* that we should fear God.

Qoholet & Meaning

So what does Qoholet mean when he says that life is meaningless? It will help to remember that he is a member of the ancient wisdom movement. He is not a modern existentialist philosopher. A number of modern philosophies argue that life is more like an onion than an avocado. Peel away the skin and flesh of an avocado and you're left with a solid core. For many people, life is like that. There is a solid core of God-given truth that should form the basis for how we construct our lives. But pick up an onion and start peeling away the layers and you eventually get to…nothing. Some modern philosophies argue that life is like the onion. Strip away the layers of your life and at the centre you'll find nothing…no god, no God-given truth. In such a world each of us needs to choose our own truth, identity and meaning.

Qoholet is not a premodern postmodernist. When he says, "Meaningless, meaningless, everything is meaningless" he is not arguing that he lives in a godless universe devoid of any God-given meaning. He has a strong belief in God and that we can live meaningfully. His argument is rather about the limits of our ability to discern the order God has placed in the universe.

The assumption of wisdom was that behaviour has consequences. Wise behaviour brings positive life outcomes and foolish behaviour invites disaster. Yet Qoholet struggles to see this principle at work. He sees many ways behaviour and reward are mismatched. For example, with much wisdom comes much sorrow (1:18); a person who amasses great wealth and achievements may be anxious about them (1:22; 5:12) or discontent with what they do have and caught up in wanting more (5:10); the righteous can perish while the wicked prosper (7:15)

Above all, death reduces everyone to the same end.

> *So I turned to consider wisdom and madness and folly; for what can the one do who comes after the king? Only what has already been done. Then I saw that wisdom excels folly as light excels darkness.*

> *The wise have eyes in their head,*
>> *but fools walk in darkness.*
>
> Yet I perceived that the same fate befalls all of them. Then I said to myself, 'What happens to the fool will happen to me also; why then have I been so very wise?' And I said to myself that this also is vanity. For there is no enduring remembrance of the wise or of fools, seeing that in the days to come all will have been long forgotten. How can the wise die just like fools? So I hated life, because what is done under the sun was grievous to me; for all is vanity and a chasing after wind.
> Ecclesiastes 2.12-17 NRSV

Qoholet did not have the hope of resurrection that we have today through Jesus. This had yet to be revealed. Rather, he understood that at death we all pass into a shadowy, semi-real existence. Ultimately righteousness and wickedness met with the same outcome, the shadowy, semi-real existence of the grave. And to make matters worse, whatever wealth one amassed may well be mismanaged by those who inherit it, and whatever one has achieved in this life will be forgotten by future generations.

It is this that leads Qoholet to the conclusion that everything is meaningless. He cannot see that the universe rewards goodness and penalises evil. In the end there is no difference in outcome for the wise and the foolish and in the present wisdom and goodness do not necessarily find reward. Whatever we pursue, the outcomes are unpredictable, rendering them and our efforts to make sense of them futile. For Qoholet wisdom, the ability to discern moral order in the universe has value, but it is limited. He is aware that life is not predictable, that bad and unpleasant things happen.

Trust God and Enjoy All You Can

Qoholet was no atheist, but was a person of deep faith. His conclusion was not that God is absent from the world, but that God's ordering of it is often beyond our understanding. In the oft quoted and hauntingly beautiful words of chapter 3, he concluded that God has ordered the world so that everything good and bad had its time and place.

> *For everything there is a season, and a time for every matter under heaven:*
>
> *a time to be born, and a time to die;*
> *a time to plant, and a time to pluck up what is planted;*
> *a time to kill, and a time to heal;*
> *a time to break down, and a time to build up;*
> *a time to weep, and a time to laugh;*
> *a time to mourn, and a time to dance;*
> *a time to throw away stones, and a time to gather stones together;*
> *a time to embrace, and a time to refrain from embracing;*
> *a time to seek, and a time to lose;*
> *a time to keep, and a time to throw away;*
> *a time to tear, and a time to sew;*
> *a time to keep silence, and a time to speak;*
> *a time to love, and a time to hate;*
> *a time for war, and a time for peace.*
>
> *What gain have the workers from their toil? I have seen the business that God has given to everyone to be busy with. He has made everything suitable for its time; moreover, he has put a sense of past and future into their minds, yet they cannot find out what God has done from the beginning to the end. I know*

that there is nothing better for them than to be happy and enjoy themselves as long as they live; moreover, it is God's gift that all should eat and drink and take pleasure in all their toil. I know that whatever God does endures for ever; nothing can be added to it, nor anything taken from it; God has done this, so that all should stand in awe before him. That which is, already has been; that which is to be, already is; and God seeks out what has gone by.
Ecclesiastes 3:1-15 NRSV

Qoholet points to the different "times" in our lives, periods when it will be appropriate to weep or tear down or throw away and periods when we experience the opposite. The problem is that we simply don't know when these times will come. God has placed a sense of the progression of time in our hearts but we struggle to know what will befall us. This ultimate type of wisdom belongs to God alone.

Rather than being paralysed by the unpredictability of life, Qoholet invites us to enjoy the good times while we can. This theme appears here and throughout the book.

There is nothing better for mortals than to eat and drink, and find enjoyment in their toil. This also, I saw, is from the hand of God; for apart from him who can eat or who can have enjoyment?
2.24-25 NRSV

So I saw that there is nothing better than that all should enjoy their work, for that is their lot; who can bring them to see what will be after them?
3:22 NRSV

This is what I have seen to be good: it is fitting to eat and drink and find enjoyment in all the toil with which one toils under the sun the few days of the life God gives us; for this is our lot. Likewise all to whom God gives wealth and possessions and whom he enables to enjoy them, and to accept their lot and find enjoyment in their toil—this is the gift of God.
5:18-19 NRSV

Go, eat your bread with enjoyment, and drink your wine with a merry heart; for God has long ago approved what you do. Let your garments always be white; do not let oil be lacking on your head. Enjoy life with the wife whom you love, all the days of your vain life that are given you under the sun, because that is your portion in life and in your toil at which you toil under the sun.
9:7-9 NRSV

When my children were young, summer meant trips to the beach and the construction of sandcastles. The experience brought Qoholet's wisdom home to me. We created castles of often gigantic proportions. We collected seaweed, shells and driftwood that would be transformed in our imagination into flags and drawbridges and various items of furniture. We invented stories about the kings and queens who lived in our castle. We dug moats around the castle and trenches stretching toward the surf to allow incoming waves to fill the moat. We lived fully in those moments, thrilled to be alive, full of laughter and dreams.

After we left the beach the rising tide would wash our castle away, erasing all evidence of our having been there. But that didn't matter, for in the short time we were there we laughed and played, we imagined other worlds into being, we enjoyed the softness of the sand beneath our feet, the warmth of the sun upon our faces and the cool rush of the waves around our ankles. Above all, we enjoyed each other.

Qoholet suggests life is like this. Generations come and go, each of them relatively insignificant in the grand scheme of things, but oh, what exquisite pleasure can be found in God's earth along the way. Yes, there will be difficulties and sorrows, but there will also be pleasures and joys; pleasures and joys to be received as the gift of God.

Living It Out

The Book of Ecclesiastes provides profound and unique insight into living well through suffering. As in the story of Job, we are reminded that life cannot be reduced to simple platitudes. Reality has been severely distorted by sin. The selfish, proud and pushy often get what they seek, while the loving, humble and servant-hearted often do not. The powerful often ruthlessly exploit the weak. The wicked prosper while the righteous go hungry. Life can be terribly unpredictable and unfair.

The question is how we will live with its unpredictability. Qoholet's answer is to build sandcastles. There will be times to weep, mourn and break down, but there will also be times to laugh, dance and build. It is possible the writer simply wants us to see all these times as coming from the hand of God. Alternately, Qoholet may be arguing that God places limits on evil and dysfunction. God will not allow war, mourning, death and hatred to dominate his universe, but has ordered the world so that they run their course and are vanquished by peace, laughter, life and love.

So enjoy the good times as the gift of God. Qoholet is not an ascetic who denies himself pleasure. Rather, enjoying what God has given is one of the things that makes life bearable. Hold dinner parties, climb mountains, build sandcastles, and do it all while "fearing God". It's all too easy to get so caught up with the busyness of life that we miss its joy. Make space to stop and smell the roses. Receive the pleasures of life as the gift of God.

Questions for Reflection

1. In the last 12 months what are the things that have brought you satisfaction and joy?

2. Throughout the book Qoholet is frustrated by the fact that he knows there is an order to the world – a time to laugh and a tome to cry; a time to mend and a time to throw away - but he has no way of knowing when those times will fall upon him and whether they will be joyful or painful. Can you identify with this? How has it shaped your life and faith?

3. We don't often think of taking time to do that which gives us joy as a spiritual discipline. What are the ways this could help you deal with life's challenges? How might you build this into your life?

A Prayer

My God,
Thank you for the little joys in life.
For the song of birds
The laughter of children
The cool touch of water on a stinking hot day
The joy of a meal shared with friends
For the way I get lost in a story
For the sensation of grass beneath my bare feet
For the embrace of someone who loves me
For the joke that makes me laugh until I cry
Even as life crashes in around me
and my world faces seemingly insurmountable challenges
help me never to forget to make the space in my life
for the simple pleasures
and to receive them as a gift.

Chapter Six

Ruth. The Welcoming Arms of Community

Call me no longer Naomi [which means 'pleasant'],
 call me Mara [which means 'bitter'],
 for the Almighty has dealt bitterly with me.
I went away full,
 but the LORD has brought me back empty;
why call me Naomi
 when the LORD has dealt harshly with me,
 and the Almighty has brought calamity upon me?'

Homecomings are supposed to be joyous, festive occasions; a time for the outpouring of happiness; for excitement at seeing one another face to face; for the telling of tales and the reliving of memories. This however was no such homecoming. This homecoming was etched in sorrow, more bitter than sweet. It's a homecoming story told in the book of Ruth, and one that has much to teach about the value of community in helping us cope when life falls in around us.

The Lord Has Turned Against Me

The book of Ruth recounts the story of an Israelite woman,

Naomi, and her Moabite daughter-in-law Ruth. Naomi and her husband had migrated to Moab, where they raised their family and their sons married Moabite women. We enter the story when tragedy had struck. Naomi's husband and sons have died.

These women were hit with a double blow. On the one hand, there was the grief of losing their husbands, and in Naomi's case her husband and children. On the other hand, there was the extremely precarious situation widowhood created for them. Theirs was a world where power and influence were exercised by men. Without a man to protect her interests a widow was extremely vulnerable to poverty, abuse and exploitation. Naomi's daughters-in-law had the possibility of returning to the protection of their father's homes and were young enough to remarry, but Naomi was old and a foreigner in Moab. As she peered into her future, all she could see was difficulty and despair.

Deciding her only hope was a return to her home country, Naomi urged her daughters-in-law to return to their families of origin. One of them, Ruth, refused. She will not abandon her mother-in-law.

> *Where you go, I will go;*
> *where you lodge, I will lodge;*
> *your people shall be my people,*
> *and your God my God.*
> *Where you die, I will die—*
> *there will I be buried.*
> *May the* LORD *do thus and so to me,*
> *and more as well,*
> *if even death parts me from you!*
> Ruth 1.16-17 NRSV

It was an extraordinary act of loyalty and love. Despite the fact that Naomi was an elderly widow with few prospects for her future, in order to care for her Ruth gave up the relative security of her father's household and the likelihood of a secure future for herself. She would be a foreigner in Israel and without a male to protect her interests.

As might be expected, Naomi's return generated excitement. The women who had bid her farewell a decade or more previously could scarcely believe she had returned, but Naomi would not tolerate celebration.

> *Call me no longer Naomi [which means 'pleasant'],*
>   *call me Mara [which means 'bitter'],*
>   *for the Almighty has dealt bitterly with me.*
> *I went away full,*
>   *but the LORD has brought me back empty;*
> *why call me Naomi*
>   *when the LORD has dealt harshly with me,*
>   *and the Almighty has brought calamity upon me?'*
> Ruth 1.20-21 NRSV

Naomi was stuck inside her grief, depressed, bitter, and convinced God had made her life miserable.

Yet as bleak was the outlook for Naomi, it was worse for Ruth. At least Naomi had friends and family. Ruth had only Naomi, who was so wrapped up in her grief that she didn't acknowledge the blessing Ruth was to her.

The Power Of Community

When Israel was constituted as God's people, God gave guidelines to ensure that those who were vulnerable, such as widows, were included in the life of the community and provision made for their needs. One of these provisions concerned the harvest. Landowners were to leave the edges of their fields unharvested and to make only one sweep of the remainder of their fields. Those who were poor were free to harvest the edges and do the second and subsequent sweeps.

A second provision was the law of levirate marriage. According to this law a woman who was widowed before she had given birth to a son was to marry her brother-in-law with whom she would have a child who bore her deceased husband's name and would inherit his land. This had two important consequences. First, it ensured that family lines would continue, something that was highly valued in the ancient world. Second, it brought the widow under the protection of an adult male and secured her on the land she and her deceased husband had shared.

This law is abhorrent to Western minds, where marriage is undertaken for love and individual freedom is valued above all else. In the context of the Ancient Near East however, where marriage served predominantly social functions and women's rights were severely limited, the law of levirate marriage could be an important source of security for a widow such as Ruth.

But would these provisions of community be applied to Ruth? Not only was she a foreigner, but the story is set in the period of the Judges. This was a time of spiritual decline in Israel in which idolatry and disregard for the law of God was common.

Gleaning in the Fields of Boaz

Now Naomi had a kinsman on her husband's side, a prominent rich man, of the family of Elimelech, whose name was Boaz. And Ruth the Moabite said to Naomi, 'Let me go to the field and glean among the ears of grain, behind someone in whose sight I may find favour.' She said to her, 'Go, my daughter.' So she went. She came and gleaned in the field behind the reapers. As it happened, she came to the part of the field belonging to Boaz, who was of the family of Elimelech. Just then Boaz came from Bethlehem. He said to the reapers, 'The LORD be with you.' They answered, 'The LORD bless you.' Then Boaz said to his servant who was in charge of the reapers, 'To whom does this young woman belong?' The servant who was in charge of the reapers answered, 'She is the Moabite who came back with Naomi from the country of Moab. She said, "Please let me glean and gather among the sheaves behind the reapers." So she came, and she has been on her feet from early this morning until now, without resting even for a moment.'

Then Boaz said to Ruth, 'Now listen, my daughter, do not go to glean in another field or leave this one, but keep close to my young women. Keep your eyes on the field that is being reaped, and follow behind them. I have ordered the young men not to bother you. If you get thirsty, go to the vessels and drink from what the young men have drawn.' Then she fell prostrate, with her face to the ground, and said to him, 'Why have I found favour in your sight, that you should take notice of me, when I am a foreigner?' But Boaz answered her, 'All that you have done for your mother-in-law since the death of your husband has been fully told me, and how you left your father and mother and your native land and came to a people that you did not know before. May the LORD reward you for your deeds, and may you have a full reward from the LORD, the God of Israel, under whose wings you have come for refuge!'

Ruth 2:1-12 NRSV

Aware of the laws of gleaning, Ruth the Moabite entered a field and joined the harvesting. She was unsure how she would be received, but was fortunate that she was in the field of Boaz, a good man, who assured her she was welcome, instructed his staff not to harass her, and even to leave sheaves for Ruth. Boaz had heard about Ruth and the devotion she had shown to her embittered mother-in-law and he was impressed. In distinct contrast to Naomi who declared God had made her life bitter, Boaz declared that Ruth had been blessed by the God of Israel, "under whose wings you have come for refuge."

At the Threshing Floor of Boaz

What of the possibility of marriage? Naomi's sons were dead, so the responsibility to marry Ruth and have a child who would take his deceased father's name fell to a close relative. Both Naomi and Ruth hoped it would be Boaz. In a custom clouded by time, Ruth dressed in her finest clothes and went to the threshing room where Boaz had been working. After a hard day's work, a big meal and not a few drinks, Boaz had lain down to sleep. Ruth clandestinely slipped into the room, uncovered his feet and lay down at them. She waited some time, very nervously I imagine, until Boaz woke. Naomi had instructed Ruth to do whatever Boaz asked, and there is little doubt a less scrupulous man might take sexual advantage, but not Boaz. The account is almost comic:

> *At midnight the man was startled and turned over, and there, lying at his feet, was a woman.*
> Ruth 3:8 NRSV

Boaz instantly recognized that Naomi was asking him to fulfil the role of near relative by marrying her and he was overjoyed!

How both their hopes were dashed when Boaz reluctantly acknowledged there was a closer relative than he. Custom demanded that the closest relative be the one with first responsibility to marry a widow.

Boaz was now a man on a mission. He spoke to the close relative, who was keen to get access to Naomi's land but, when he discovered it meant taking Ruth as his wife and sharing his estate with the children they might have, he surrendered the responsibility of nearest relative to Boaz.

In the Line of Kings

Boaz and Ruth married and had a son who later became the grandfather of King David. In keeping with the book's emphasis on Naomi, the women of Bethlehem celebrate that through Boaz and Ruth Naomi regained the children she had lost and would now be secure in her old age.

> *So Boaz took Ruth and she became his wife. When they came together, the LORD made her conceive, and she bore a son. Then the women said to Naomi, 'Blessed be the LORD, who has not left you this day without next-of-kin; and may his name be renowned in Israel! He shall be to you a restorer of life and a nourisher of your old age; for your daughter-in-law who loves you, who is more to you than seven sons, has borne him.' Then Naomi took the child and laid him in her bosom, and became his nurse. The women of the neighbourhood gave him a name, saying, 'A son has been born to Naomi.' They named him Obed; he became the father of Jesse, the father of David.*
> Ruth 4:13-16 NRSV

The book closes on an entirely different note to its beginning. In chapter one we saw two women whose life situation was precarious, whose future was bleak, and who, in Naomi's case, was bitter. By the end of the book they were secure, the future was hopeful, and their hearts were thankful.

The reason for this transformation was the functioning of healthy community, embodied in the character of Boaz. Boaz acted with generosity, grace and goodness, fulfilling the Law in both letter and spirit. As a result, the most vulnerable in the community, a foreign widow and an elderly widow, "found refuge under the wings of God".

Community & Suffering

One of the key messages of the story is that healthy community enables people to cope with life's challenges. In the story of Ruth and Naomi we see what happened when Boaz took seriously the call of the Old Testament Law to open his fields up to the poor and to assume the close relative responsibility to provide protection to the widow.

These were but two examples of a principle of care that lay at the heart of the Old Testament Law. The Law recognised that difficult times would come to people. A woman would be widowed, a farmer's crop would fail, a day labourer would not find work. Rather than being left to fend for themselves, the Law provided instruction in how the members of the community could care for one another.

In the New Testament the theme is continued. We are to love one another, to bear each other's burdens, to encourage and build up one another, to teach and admonish one another. When we see someone hungry we are to feed her; when someone is sick we are to visit him;

when someone has sinned against us we are to forgive.

This is much more than superficiality, where we have many acquaintances but few friends. It's a call to robust community in which people find assistance when they face material difficulty, emotional support when they are emotionally wounded, and spiritual support as they seek to follow the way of Jesus.

Living It Out

How then do we live this out? I have three suggestions. First we need to be humble enough to receive care. One of the great myths of the middle class westerner is that we are self-made and self-sufficient. This often makes it difficult for us to receive care.

I have noticed this within myself as the symptoms of Parkinson's set in. I sometimes need help buttoning up my left sleeve on a business shirt. The first time I asked Sandy to do it was quite difficult. It was an admission of lost competency. I had to swallow my pride if I was to receive care. And I'm glad I did, for it was provided with grace, generosity and love. I think it made me more human.

Second, we need to be patient with each other. When people face severe difficulties their emotional energy can be fully expended on simply coping. They may demand a lot from us but offer little in return. They might withdraw. They might become unreliable. But it's at these times that they need us most.

Third, we need to be available to care. I find that one of the greatest impediments to my caring for others is busyness. I have every intention of ringing or visiting, but days and even weeks can pass before I carve out space to turn my feelings of concern into concrete actions of care. I wonder if we should not make a habit of carving out five minutes every day to make a phone call, write a note, or send an email to someone who needs our love?

For Naomi healthy community was the difference between disaster and coping, between despair and hope. I suspect the same holds true for us today.

Questions for Reflection

1. What are your most powerful experiences of supportive community? What were the circumstances and what did people do that caused you to feel valued and supported?

2. The story of Ruth and Naomi is set in the period of the Judges, when many Israelites were turning away from Yahweh to idols and away from one another and the systems of care God gave them. Boaz however remained faithful to God's call to community and it made all the difference to Ruth and Naomi. What is the nature of community our churches should have? In what ways does God call us to build into each other's lives?

3. Identify one or two people in your network of relationships who are experiencing difficulty. What could you/your group do this week to support them?

A Prayer

God of lovingkindness

Thankyou for the people who
step into my world
and offer me
the gifts of their
presence
empathy
compassion
love
understanding
patience
grace
friendship

In their presence I sense your presence
in their empathy your empathy
in their compassion your compassion
in their love your love
in their understanding your understanding
in their patience your patience
in their grace your grace
in their friendship your friendship.

Chapter Seven

Paul. The Fringe Benefits of Suffering

In 2006 JK Rowling, author of the Harry Potter series of books, gave a speech to the graduating students at Harvard University. In the lead up to the speech Rowling agonised over what she might share. She asked herself what she wished she had known on her graduation day twenty-one years earlier, which led her to deliver an extraordinary speech on "the benefits of failure...and the critical importance of imagination."

Rowling described her post university plunge into the abyss of failure. Just seven years after graduating, JK Rowling was not the successful author we know today, but an unemployed single parent with a failed marriage behind her. It was a sad and dark period in her life, yet wrapped up inside failure was an unexpected blessing. Rowling found that failure stripped away all her pretentions and illusions about herself and forced her to focus on what she really wanted to achieve with her life. It was out of this painful period that the Harry Potter books emerged.

JK Rowling's experience is not unique. Time and time again those who suffer find that in ways completely unexpected their suffering becomes an occasion of blessing. It's not that the suffering is good, nor that the pain is lessened, but that in the midst of the suffering is an occasion for growth and transformation.

Just as JK Rowling spoke of "the benefits of failure", so the Bible speaks of the benefits of suffering. Yes, suffering is an ugly and unwanted intrusion into God's good world. Yes, it is an enemy to be defeated. But whether it's dashed hopes, broken relationships, physical disability, poor health, or some other form of life challenge, the bible operates with the conviction that there are blessings to be found within your pain.

A Thorn in the Flesh

In 2 Corinthians 12 the apostle Paul described a permanent, painful and most likely embarrassing physical condition he endured. In ways very similar to JK Rowling's reflection on failure, he spoke of the ways this had been beneficial for him.

> *It is necessary to boast; nothing is to be gained by it, but I will go on to visions and revelations of the Lord. I know a person in Christ who fourteen years ago was caught up to the third heaven—whether in the body or out of the body I do not know; God knows. And I know that such a person—whether in the body or out of the body I do not know; God knows— was caught up into Paradise and heard things that are not to be told, that no mortal is permitted to repeat. On behalf of such a one I will boast, but on my own behalf I will not boast, except of my weaknesses. But if I wish to boast, I will not be a fool, for I will be speaking the truth. But I refrain from it, so that no one may think better of me than what is seen in me or heard from me, even considering the exceptional character of the revelations. Therefore, to keep me from being too elated, a thorn was given to me in the flesh, a messenger of Satan to torment me, to keep me*

> *from being too elated. Three times I appealed to the Lord about this, that it would leave me, but he said to me, 'My grace is sufficient for you, for power is made perfect in weakness.' So, I will boast all the more gladly of my weaknesses, so that the power of Christ may dwell in me. Therefore I am content with weaknesses, insults, hardships, persecutions, and calamities for the sake of Christ; for whenever I am weak, then I am strong.*
> 2 Corinthians 12:1-10 NRSV

For many years the narrative around Paul suggested that before his conversion to Christ he was a man wracked by guilt. An extremely devout Hebrew, he did everything he could to earn God's favour, but the more he tried the more acutely he was aware of his failures. His sense of worthlessness was resolved only when he discovered that faith in Christ and this alone made him right with God.

This narrative most likely reflects the experiences of later generations read back onto Paul. It appears from his letters that far from being wracked with guilt and self-doubt, Paul was a highly driven man who had a tendency to pride. In Philippians 3, for example, he described his life before coming to faith in Christ like this:

> *If anyone else has reason to be confident in the flesh, I have more: circumcised on the eighth day, a member of the people of Israel, of the tribe of Benjamin, a Hebrew born of Hebrews; as to the law, a Pharisee; as to zeal, a persecutor of the church; as to righteousness under the law, blameless.*
> Philippians 3:4-6 NRSV

This text suggests that the pre-conversion Paul was convinced of his own righteousness. As a devout Jew Paul will have lived with three defining realities: the Law, which guided his behaviour; the Temple, where the sacrificial system made atonement for his sin; and the Land, which God gave his people. Within this framework Paul argues that he was the very embodiment of faithfulness to God. One of the pre-eminent Pharisees of his time, filled with zeal for God and devoted to observing God's law, he was convinced that he was righteous and blameless before God.

While his encounter with Christ certainly changed this view of himself, the tendency to pride remained. In the passage we are considering he speaks of an extraordinary vision experience. He was caught up into the heavens where he was privy to things unknown to mere mortals. Rather than humbling him, it was possible this experience would make him arrogant and proud, fill him with a sense of his own spiritual depth. So we read, "to keep me from being too elated, a thorn was given to me in the flesh."

Scholars speculate about the precise nature of the thorn. It is generally agreed that it most likely made him unimpressive as a public figure. Was it a speech impediment? Recurring bouts of malaria? A disfigurement? We don't know and don't need to know. What matters is that it served to curb his pride. In his second letter to the Corinthians Paul was battling a group of "super apostles", teachers who came to Corinth with false ideas but impressive rhetorical skills. Clever argument was highly prized, and the false apostles were winning many over. Paul by contrast appeared weak and insubstantial. Yet, Paul reflects, when he engaged in his mission it was evident that God spoke through him. His weakness magnified God's greatness.

Significantly, while Paul appreciated the benefit the thorn had in his life, he described it as a "messenger of Satan" and three times asked God to remove it from him. It was something that belonged to the fallenness of our world, something from which God would one day redeem him. In the hands of God, however, it became a tool to grow him as a person, to curb his pride.

> *Three times I appealed to the Lord about this, that it would leave me, but he said to me, 'My grace is sufficient for you, for power is made perfect in weakness.'* NRSV

Paul's Other Sufferings

Paul's thorn in the flesh, whatever it may have been, was not the only way he suffered. Just before he spoke of this thorn he catalogued the hardships he'd experienced in his service of the Gospel.

> *But whatever anyone dares to boast of—I am speaking as a fool—I also dare to boast of that. Are they Hebrews? So am I. Are they Israelites? So am I. Are they descendants of Abraham? So am I. Are they ministers of Christ? I am talking like a madman—I am a better one: with far greater labours, far more imprisonments, with countless floggings, and often near death. Five times I have received from the Jews the forty lashes minus one. Three times I was beaten with rods. Once I received a stoning. Three times I was shipwrecked; for a night and a day I was adrift at sea; on frequent journeys, in danger from rivers, danger from bandits, danger from my own people, danger from Gentiles, danger in the city, danger in the wilderness, danger at sea, danger from false brothers and sisters; in toil and hardship, through many a sleepless night, hungry and thirsty, often without food, cold and naked. And, besides other things, I am under daily pressure because of my anxiety for all the churches. Who is weak, and I am not weak? Who is made to stumble, and I am not indignant?*

> *If I must boast, I will boast of the things that show my weakness. The God and Father of the Lord Jesus (blessed be he for ever!) knows that I do not lie. In Damascus, the governor under King Aretas set a guard on the city of Damascus in order to[g] seize me, but I was let down in a basket through a window in the wall, and escaped from his hands…*
>
> *So, I will boast all the more gladly of my weaknesses, so that the power of Christ may dwell in me. Therefore I am content with weaknesses, insults, hardships, persecutions, and calamities for the sake of Christ; for whenever I am weak, then I am strong.*
> 2 Corinthians 11:21-12:10 NRSV

The lesson he had learned through the thorn in the flesh he experienced as a general principle of life. His opponents at Corinth disparaged him, suggested he did not display the hallmarks of a true apostle. Paul insisted he more than matched them, but took the argument in what appears to be an absurd direction. Rather than talking about his greatness, he preferred to talk about his weakness and inadequacy, for it was at these points that the grace and power of God were most evident in his life.

Earlier in his letter to the Corinthians he made the same point

> *For we do not proclaim ourselves; we proclaim Jesus Christ as Lord and ourselves as your slaves for Jesus' sake. For it is the God who said, 'Let light shine out of darkness', who has shone in our hearts to give the light of the knowledge of the glory of God in the face of Jesus Christ.*
>
> *But we have this treasure in clay jars, so that it may be made clear that this extraordinary power belongs to God and does not come from us. We are afflicted in every way, but not crushed;*

> *perplexed, but not driven to despair; persecuted, but not forsaken; struck down, but not destroyed; always carrying in the body the death of Jesus, so that the life of Jesus may also be made visible in our bodies.*
> 2 Corinthians 4:5-10 NRSV

It was not impressive rhetoric nor exalted status that made the gospel effective. Rather it was the power of the message itself, the fact that God spoke in and through him. For Paul suffering, as painful as it may have been, was an opportunity to experience the grace of God working through him to benefit others.

The Fringe Benefits of Suffering

In Romans 5 Paul talks about the positive impacts suffering can play for all of us.

> *Therefore, since we have been justified through faith, we have peace with God through our Lord Jesus Christ, through whom we have gained access by faith into this grace in which we now stand. And we boast in the hope of the glory of God. Not only so, but we also glory in our sufferings, because we know that suffering produces perseverance; perseverance, character; and character, hope. And hope does not put us to shame, because God's love has been poured out into our hearts through the Holy Spirit, who has been given to us.*
> Romans 5:1-5 NRSV

Suffering is the first step in a chain of personal transformation. Suffering, says Paul, produces perseverance, the capacity to keep going even though it's tough. Perseverance produces character, the knowledge of who one is and what one stands for. Character produces hope, for knowing who we are and what we stand for in

Christ drives us to live in light of the coming kingdom. Here is the fringe benefit of suffering.

I frequently hear this from people who have experienced suffering, often extreme suffering. They find themselves shaped by it. They learn things about themselves and God that they never appreciated before. They discover a resilience they did not know they possessed. They develop a greater depth of empathy and compassion for those who suffer. Would they wish their suffering on their worst enemy? No. Their suffering is painful, but nonetheless it proves an opportunity for incredible personal growth.

One of the most vivid examples came when Sandy and I were invited to a 40th birthday party of a friend who was an alcoholic. I dreaded the thought of going, for it was one of those parties where we would know nobody else. It turned out to be one of the most immensely rewarding experiences I have had. Everybody else at the party bar Sandy and I was a recovering alcoholic. Every one of them had hit rock bottom, done things they were embarrassed about and ashamed of, and had come out the other side. They were free of pretense and were gifted with a remarkable openness to one another and to outsiders such as Sandy and I. We came away feeling we had experienced what true community should be like. Genuine welcome, sincere acceptance of one another, including one another's gifts and faults, a deep humility, and a determination to grab this second chance at life with both hands. Not one of them would ever wish upon another person what they had been through. Yet their experience of suffering gave them a strength of character I could but envy.

My own experience with Parkinson's has been a discovery of the generosity of others, to learn humility, and a renewed sense of trust in God. I have been deeply touched by the generosity of close friends and the kindness of strangers. It has been a difficult thing losing my independence. Having to ask somebody to do up a button, to open a bag of chips, to bait a fish hook, or to carry a drink for me has assaulted my sense of competence and been deeply humbling. I had not understood the depth to which I had imbibed the middle-class Anglo belief in self-reliance. I have found and still find it difficult to ask people for help. Yet at every point I have discovered both friends and strangers more than willing to provide assistance. In an entirely unexpected way I have discovered my humanity and I think have helped draw out the humanity of others. We are at our best when we are giving and receiving love.

Likewise, my hope and trust in God have deepened. No longer is the doctrine of the resurrection of all believers merely a piece of the furniture of my mind. It has become a comfy armchair in which I take rest. The hope of a transformed body has become very real, which in turn drives home to me hope of transformation in every part of me.

Living It Out

Growth through suffering is not automatic. Where some people grow, others only suffer. Growth comes only as we accept that an evil has fallen upon us but that God can use it to grow us. This does not mean pretending that our suffering is a good. Injustice, disease, disability, relationship breakdown, financial ruin, are not good. But they can become an instrument for good in our lives. They can shape our character and our impact in the world in ways that never would otherwise have occurred. This is the fringe benefit of suffering.

Questions for Reflection

1. In a commencement address at Harvard University, JK Rowling spoke of the benefits of failure. How have experiences of failure brought unexpected growth into your life?

2. Read Romans 5:1-5. How have you seen adversity produce perseverance (the patient determination to follow the way of Jesus), character (qualities such as love, joy, peace, patience, kindness, etc that marked Jesus) and hope (anticipation of life in the new heavens and earth) in your life or the life of others?

3. A wise person once noted that where some 60 year olds have 60 years of experience, some have had one year's experience 60 times over. Suffering does not automatically produce growth. What attitudes and actions do you need to cultivate in order to grow through suffering? Of the items in your list, which is the strongest and which the weakest? How can you continue to cultivate you strengths and address your weak areas?

A Prayer

God over all,
It is just like you to take something that shouldn't be
and use it to shape me into what I should be.

I don't welcome suffering,
this alien intrusion that brings chaos
and disorder to your good world.
But I do welcome the opportunity to grow through suffering.

As I navigate this period of my life
grant me the grace to do so
without bitterness.
I want to be teachable, to find the unexpected benefit of suffering
Teach me, refine me, mould me, change me.

Chapter Eight

John. The Final Healing

"If you want a picture of the future, imagine a boot stamping on a human face – forever."

This chilling sentence is found in George Orwell's novel *Nineteen Eighty-Four*. Orwell imagines a world under the control of authoritarian regimes, where the State controls where people live, what they do, where they work, what they say, even how they think. "Thought crime", to think thoughts that are against the ideology of the Party, is a heinous wrong.

The central character in Orwell's book is a man named Winston, who works at the Ministry of Truth, rewriting history so that it fits with the regime's view of the world. He despises what he does and the regime that makes him do it. Winston begins rebelling. He engages in small but deliberate acts of defiance: he finds an alcove in his house where the cameras cannot observe him; he begins an illicit affair with a woman named Julia; and in his own thoughts he questions the way the world is. Each small act of rebellion increases the likelihood Winston will be caught.

The tension rises until the fateful moment when Winston's resistance is exposed. He is sent to prison to be "rehabilitated". This means breaking him emotionally and physically and then turning him once more into a party drone. His interrogator, O'Brien, wants to convince Winston that resistance is futile, that the Party will never be defeated, that the present will stretch unending into the future. At one point O'Brien chillingly says to Winston: "If you want a picture of the future, imagine a boot stamping on a human face – forever."

It can feel like this to all of us who suffer; that suffering, pain and oppression are here with us forever.

To this the gospel screams a loud "NO!" It declares that death, disease and distress will not be the last word, that the risen Christ will return to restore the universe to goodness and justice. This is the Christian hope.

Exile & Persecution

It is the message of the Book of Revelation. Often the subject of speculative interpretation and end of the world predictions, the book of Revelation is nothing more and nothing less than a declaration of the victory of God over evil. It opens with the apostle John living in exile on the island of Patmos. His is an Orwellian world. A wave of persecution had broken out against the Christians. The Roman government, described in Romans 13 as a servant of God, had become a ferocious beast, tearing apart all who refused to worship the emperor.

John employed a style of writing we refer to as "apocalyptic". It is completely unlike anything we are used to reading. Apocalyptic literature does not use straightforward prose but describes the world using dramatic symbolism. An oppressive government is pictured as a ferocious wild animal of gigantic proportions; significant events on earth are matched by cataclysmic events in the heavens, such as stars falling from the sky; the contest between good and evil is pictured as an almighty battle between an army led by God and armies led by

Satan.

In chapter 13 John describes the Roman Imperial government as a frightening and grotesque beast rising out of the sea. It resembles a leopard but its feet are like those of the bear and its mouth like that of a lion. The beast wields authority over all humankind, sets itself against God, and makes war upon the followers of Jesus.

Most scholars think John writes during the reign of either Nero or Domitian, both known for persecuting Christians. Nero, for example, was a madman during whose reign a great fire swept through the city of Rome. When suspicions grew that the fire was deliberately started by the Emperor, he took the opportunity to blame it on the Christians, already despised because of their refusal to worship the gods of the city. The historian Tacitus described the extraordinary cruelty with which Nero inflicted "punishment" upon Christians:

> *Nero fastened the guilt and inflicted the most exquisite tortures on a class hated for their abominations, called Christians by the populace. Christus, from whom the name had its origin, suffered the extreme penalty during the reign of Tiberius at the hands of one of our procurators, Pontius Pilatus, and a most mischievous superstition, thus checked for the moment, again broke out not only in Judaea, the first source of the evil, but even in Rome, where all things hideous and shameful from every part of the world find their centre and become popular. Accordingly, an arrest was first made of all who pleaded guilty; then, upon their information, an immense multitude was convicted, not so much of the crime of firing the city, as of hatred against mankind. Mockery of every sort was added to their deaths. Covered with the skins of beasts, they were torn by dogs and perished, or were nailed to crosses, or were doomed to the flames and burnt, to*

serve as a nightly illumination, when daylight had expired.
Tacitus, *Annals* 15.44

The Scroll of Destiny

It's against a background such as this that John writes. In true apocalyptic style John is taken into heaven where he sees God seated upon a spectacularly decorated throne surrounded by twenty-four elders dressed in white robes. Six-winged creatures fly around the room declaring "holy, holy is the Lord who was, and is, and is to come." Peals of thunder and flashes of lightning emanate from the throne. The magnificence and splendour of Rome pales against the magnificence and splendour of the true God and King. It is here, not Rome, that the destiny of the world will be set.

John sees a scroll in the hand of God. The scroll has writing on both sides and has seven wax seals. The writing most likely describes the world made new. But to get there, to enact what is written on the scroll, each of the seven seals must be broken and the scroll unfurled. It dawns on John that there is no one who is worthy to take the scroll from the hand of God, break the seals, and bring history to its conclusion. He breaks down. His heaving sobs give expression to the weight of pain and terror he and his fellow Christians have endured. If the seals are unbroken the contents of the scroll cannot be read and the future will be an endless rerun of the present, of beastly powers that persecute believers, exploit the poor, and trample down the weak.

Through his tears John hears the voice of one of the elders, comforting him with the news that there is one worthy to break the seals, the crucified and risen Christ.

> *Then I saw between the throne and the four living creatures and among the elders a Lamb standing as if it had been slaughtered...*
> Revelation 5:5-6 NRSV

There is a champion; there is one who can take on the forces of evil and conquer. And when John turns to see him, he sees the most unlikely of heroes, "a Lamb standing as if it had been slaughtered." He sees the crucified but resurrected Jesus, the One who has conquered death; the One who took on every evil that could be flung at him, met it with love and grace, and rose to a new life.

Christ takes the scroll and breaks the seals one by one. As each seal is broken a particular set of events happens on earth. When the first seal is broken an armed and crowned rider appears atop a white horse. He comes out "conquering and to conquer." With the breaking of the second seal comes a red horse and its rider takes peace from the earth, causing people to slaughter each other. The third seal is broken and out comes a rider on a black horse, bringing famine. A fourth, pale horse appears with the breaking of the fourth seal.

> *Its rider was named Death, and Hades was following close behind him. They were given power over a fourth of the earth to kill by sword, famine and plague, and by the wild beasts of the earth.*
> Revelation 6:8 NRSV.

These horsemen symbolise a period of conflict and natural disaster on the earth. The focus shifts when the fifth seal is broken.

> *When he opened the fifth seal, I saw under the altar the souls of those who had been slaughtered for the word of God and for the*

> *testimony they had given; they cried out with a loud voice,*
> *'Sovereign Lord, holy and true, how long will it be before you*
> *judge and avenge our blood on the inhabitants of the earth?'*
> Revelation 6:9-10 NRSV

Outbreaks of State persecution of Christians were rare in the early history of the Church, but when they did occur they were bloody. As we have noted, it was during a period of persecution that John wrote. And so his vision includes martyrs, those who were killed on account of their faith, crying out for justice. In their minds the boot had been stamping on the human face far too long, and they pleaded with God to remove it.

The breaking of the sixth seal brings about the dissolution of the earth. The stars fall to earth, the sun turns black, the sky is rolled away. The day the martyrs long for has arrived. The time has come when Christ will judge the world.

And then, finally, the seventh seal is broken and there is silence in heaven for half an hour. Some interpreters see it as a lull before the storm. The book goes on to speak of seven trumpets sounding and seven bowls being poured out. As with the seven seals, each trumpet blast and each bowl poured out heralds suffering and destruction. Some understand these to be second and third waves of suffering and pain. Another group of interpreters see the seven trumpets and bowls as simply another way of describing the realities pictured by the seven seals. The silence in heaven at the breaking of the seventh seal is no lull before a storm, but the hushed breath of all creation as the moment to which history has been moving has finally arrived. After all the pain, all the war, all the hunger, all the suffering, the world is to be made new. The scroll is now to be unfolded and its contents read.

Whether the seven seals that are broken, trumpets sounded and bowls that are poured out represent three descriptions of the same set of events or are taken to represent three successive waves of history, the point remains the same. History is filled with oppression, violence, suffering, and pain, but it will reach a point where these have exhausted themselves, where God will finally judge evil once and for all and a new world will be inaugurated.

A New World

And so we are brought to the new creation described in the closing chapters of Revelation:

> *Then I saw a new heaven and a new earth; for the first heaven and the first earth had passed away, and the sea was no more. And I saw the holy city, the new Jerusalem, coming down out of heaven from God, prepared as a bride adorned for her husband. And I heard a loud voice from the throne saying,*
>
> *'See, the home of God is among mortals.*
> *He will dwell with them;*
> *they will be his peoples,*
> *and God himself will be with them;*
> *he will wipe every tear from their eyes.*
> *Death will be no more;*
> *mourning and crying and pain will be no more,*
> *for the first things have passed away.'*
>
> *And the one who was seated on the throne said, 'See, I am making all things new.'*
> Revelation 21:1-5 NRSV

John develops the vision of salvation found throughout the Old

Testament prophets. It is not a vision of souls leaving their bodies to ascend to a spiritual realm of heaven, but of heaven coming to earth and remaking it. In this recreated world we will have new bodies, new hearts, new minds. No longer will disease and death and genetic dysfunction mar our lives.

In this recreated world there will be no war, no famine, no violence, no oppressor, no tsunami, no earthquake, no cyclone, no flood.

In this recreated world God will be present in a much more tangible way; God's love will radiate to all creation; God's wisdom will light up every part of creation; God's grace will wash over everything.

The capital of this new world is the new Jerusalem. Jerusalem had always been an object of hope, a symbol of the presence of God with humankind, and of humanity transformed by that presence. The historical experience had been bitterly disappointing. Jerusalem was repeatedly populated with leaders who used power to further their own advantage and oppress the poor. The city was torn down by the Romans in 70 CE, a devastating declaration of dominance that concluded an extraordinarily violent rebellion. But the hope Jerusalem represented could never be destroyed. In establishing new Jerusalem as the new global capital John signifies the beginning of an era in which violence, oppression and exploitation have ended and justice, grace, and love are the new norm.

The book of Revelation was not written to fuel speculation about the events of the end time. It declares in dramatic apocalyptic style that which the rest of the New Testament describes in much more straightforward prose: that the future will not be a rerun of the present, that Christ has risen from the dead and will remake the universe after the heart and purposes of God. The resurrection has already broken into history in Jesus and will be extended creation-wide by Jesus.

Living with Hope

In 1927, the wife of Scottish preacher Arthur Gossip died suddenly. When he returned to the pulpit he preached a sermon titled "When Life Tumbles In, What Then?" In that sermon Gossip compared life to watching a plane pass through the sky during wartime. There you are, lying on your back watching a plane fly gracefully across a brilliant sunlit blue sky when all of a sudden it is blown apart by gunfire and falls to earth a tumbling, tangled mess of metal. Only on this occasion the wreck was the tragically unexpected death of his beloved wife.

Gossip went on to explain that he didn't understand this life, but what he did know was that during this darkest period of his life he needed his faith more than ever. "You people in the sunshine may believe the faith, but we in the shadow must believe it. We have nothing else."

Arthur Gossip clung tenaciously to the same hope that inspired the martyrs under Nero. The boots that stamp on human faces are not the future. The future is the removal of those boots, the reconciling of enemies, the healing of wounds both physical and psychological, the recreation of our bodies and our planet, and the revealing of God in ways we cannot even imagine.

To all of us who suffer, hope is God's ultimate answer. My body is currently deteriorating under the strain of both Parkinson's and Leukemia, but I know that I will be healed. Yes, there may be healing in this life, but even if there is, it will be temporary. We all die.

Something else will eventually claim me. One day, however, I will experience the ultimate healing, a new body in a new world wrapped up inside the tangible presence of the love, grace, and goodness of God.

This hope doesn't diminish my suffering, but it gives it context. I have met people who are devastated by their Parkinson's, who feel that their life is over and their future nothing but a descent into vulnerability, pain and frustration. For me that is also the future, but it is only a tiny slither of my future. Beyond my decay lies a glorious future in a renewed body in a renewed world.

Hope allows us to see beyond the circumstances that currently constrain us. Hope can drive us forward through the deepest valleys and the darkest nights. Hope empowers us to live meaningfully whatever life throws at us. Hope shields us from the abyss of despair to find joy even when life caves in around us.

So lay hold of the Christian hope. It's a daring and audacious hope, but it is not grounded in wishful thinking. It is grounded rather in the reality of the resurrection of Jesus. Let it fill your imagination, mesmerise your spirit, and be the light at the end of your tunnel.

Questions for Reflection

1. German theologian Jurgen Moltmann spoke of the difference between optimism and hope. Optimism looks at the present and projects what might occur in the future as one event leads to another. Hope however looks for God to bring something good when all the evidence suggests a bad outcome. What are situations in our world today that appear hopeless? What does

hope mean for these situations?

2. When the Bible speaks of the future it doesn't imagine our spirits leaving our bodies and the earth behind for an eternity in a spiritual realm called heaven, but of God coming to earth and transforming it. We will have new bodies, hearts and minds; live in communities that are just, good and faithful; inhabit a new heavens and earth; and enjoy the very tangible presence of God. What does this hope mean for you?

3. Everybody hopes *for* something and places their hope *in* something. What are the things commonly hope for in our society and what do people trust to deliver them? What difference does it make to your ambitions, values and lifestyle that the object of Christian hope is a new heavens and earth brought into being by God?

A Prayer

God of resurrection hope
I hope one day to be free from the things that bind me
those things that bind up my heart
and keep it from loving you
those things that bind up my mind
and keep me fearful and anxious
those things that bind up my body
so that it does not do the things I will.

www.ingramcontent.com/pod-product-compliance
Lightning Source LLC
Chambersburg PA
CBHW070542300426
44113CB00011B/1764